LAW AND SOCIETY

LAW AND SOCIETY

BY

CAREY KIERSTEAD GANONG, PH.D., LL.B.
Professor Emeritus, Purdue University

and

RICHARD WARREN PEARCE, M.A., LL.B.
*Associate Professor of Business Administration
Stetson University
Member of the Florida Bar*

1965

RICHARD D. IRWIN, INC.
HOMEWOOD, ILLINOIS

First Printing, May, 1965
Second Printing, January, 1967
Third Printing, May, 1968

Library of Congress Catalog Card No. 65-20528

PRINTED IN THE UNITED STATES OF AMERICA

PREFACE

A few years ago C. K. Ganong, a college professor on the verge of retirement, and R. W. Pearce, a relatively young yet successful practicing attorney, chanced to meet. Upon becoming acquainted they discovered that they were mutually interested in the social aspects of the law; that they shared the belief that there was need for a book in this field; and that they, through training and experience, complemented each other in such a way as to bring the writing of such a book by them within the realm of possibility. They, therefore, decided to attempt it, agreeing to divide the work involved upon the basis of their respective backgrounds. C. K. Ganong would assume primary responsibility for both the philosophy involved and the writing of the text, while R. W. Pearce would be primarily responsible for all matters pertaining to the law. It was understood of course that each would assist the other and that the contributions of each would be subject to the criticisms and the approval of the other. Thus it is that *Law and Society* by Carey Kierstead Ganong and Richard Warren Pearce is now being offered to the public. This book is complete in itself but it may be, depending upon the reception given it, that it will become either Part I of a larger book or Vol. I of a short series of small books dealing with other aspects of the same subject.

TABLE OF CONTENTS

APPENDIXES

INTRODUCTION

This is a book about the law, not a law book. It deals with the reasons for and nature of man-made rules rather than with the rules themselves. It is concerned with the broad aspects of the law rather than with legal detail. Our purpose in writing it has been twofold. (1) To meet the need for a short supplementary text book dealing with the cultural aspects of the law, for use in the field of the social sciences more especially that of the law, and (2) to furnish the general reader with a short treatise to aid him in arriving at intelligent conclusions with respect to some of the problems, domestic and foreign, with which he is now faced.

As a text book, *Law and Society* is designed primarily to provoke rather than to answer questions. This is in keeping with our belief that true education is a matter of directed discovery and not a matter of rote memorization.

As a book for the general reader, *Law and Society* is intended to be wholly objective in matters other than principles. That is, it states principles leaving the application of them to present day problems to the reader. For example, it does not say what things should be or what things should not be publicly owned—it simply states some of the things to be taken into consideration when deciding this question with respect to a given article. Or again it does not say whether or not Communist China should be recognized as a sovereign state and admitted into the United Nations—it simply states the criteria by which sovereignty is determined and, as above, leaves it to the reader to apply them.

Nowhere is a conscious attempt made to sell a point of view other than that our acts reflect our beliefs and that the belief in the dignity of man as an individual is what gave rise to the sovereign society known as the United States of America, and that this society, as we know it, can endure only as long as the members of it hold said belief widely and strongly enough to make democracy work.

We hope that *Law and Society* both as a textbook and as a book for the general reader will challenge those who read it to examine and re-examine their beliefs until they know why they hold them and can explain them to others. It is only in this way that they make any worthwhile contributions to the preservation and improvement of the so-called "American Way."

In concluding, we wish to express our gratitude to both the International Association of Torch Clubs and the publishers of *The New York Times*; to the former for permission to include in Chapter 1 some material originally published in *Torch Magazine* and to the latter for the right to include in our Appendix two reports and one editorial on the Genovese murder case.

CAREY KIERSTEAD GANONG
RICHARD WARREN PEARCE

DELAND, FLORIDA
April, 1965

Chapter 1

LAW:

THE FRAMEWORK

OF SOCIETY

IDEOLOGICAL ARMAMENT

In this divided world we postulate many fronts, such as the political, the cultural, the economic, the military, and the ideological. There are no clear lines of demarcation. In fact, there is much overlapping.

All fronts are important but two are of immediate, primary concern. These are the military, of which most Americans are actively aware, and the ideological, with respect to which many are relatively uninformed and therefore somewhat apathetic.

The threat of material destruction inherent in the perfecting of atomic weapons is understood and begets action. The threat inherent in the admissions of some Americans on their release from Chinese prison camps following the Korean incident, that they, when subjected to communist propaganda, became embarrassed and uneasy has not as yet occasioned the concern it merits.

These men were not exceptional. Selected in the manner in which they are, the men serving in the armed forces of the United States constitute, at all times, a cross-section of the population. Investigation has shown the early reports of disaffection among those subjected to brainwashing by the Chinese to have been exaggerated. Nonetheless, on the basis

1

of their reactions, the conclusion is justified that, while the youths of the United States are being taught to defend their country on the battlefield, they are not being adequately prepared to defend it in the realm of thought. They are well prepared to win in physical combat when and if it comes. They are ill-equipped to win the battle of ideas which is already at hand.

Armies and armaments are of great present importance but of passing concern. Beliefs are of ultimate importance and of abiding concern. What the world is to become depends upon what the people of the world come to believe. In the last analysis, arms are but the servants of beliefs.

Battles between ideologies are not won and lost in the law books of the nations, they are won and lost in the hearts and minds of men. Man-made laws can force a man into military service, but only belief in the righteousness of the cause for which he fights can make him a hero. History abounds with instances in which an honestly believing few put to rout a doubting multitude; and what has been can be again.

Those who know why they believe are less susceptible to propaganda than those who believe blindly. That only a few American men, when confronted in Chinese prison camps with arguments they could not answer, turned communist does not negate this, while the statements of those who confessed they became embarrassed and uneasy serve to confirm it. Such embarrassment and uneasiness are akin to doubt, if they do not arise from doubt, and doubt in a matter of this kind is but the prelude to disaster.

WEAKNESS OF BLIND BELIEF

Like the men who could not answer the arguments of the Communists, most Americans believe blindly in their way of life; but blind belief is not enough. In the first place, understanding fortifies belief; and, in the second place, a blind believer cannot enlighten others with respect to his beliefs.

An American who knows why he believes in the "American Way" is not embarrassed and uneasy when subjected to a communist ideological offensive either at home or abroad. He will not argue his society is without faults, but, firm in his conviction that it is one of the best yet devised by man, he will draw upon his armament of facts to launch his own ideological counteroffensive. In this way, while members of the armed services are holding the physical front for freedom, well-informed Americans everywhere can play a part in winning the metaphysical battle upon the outcome of which the destiny of the world for the next thousand years may well depend.

The more an American knows about his country and the world, the better equipped he is to do battle against alien ideologies and to work for needed reforms at home. The value of other studies is not questioned but, inasmuch as the ideology of a society finds its most concrete expression in its legal institutions, there is no substitute for a general understanding of its law.

THE LAW AS A SOCIAL STUDY

Only those who make the study of American law their profession can hope to gain a mastery of it. But so important is it in the life of everyone that no one can rightly claim to be educated in the broad sense who has no understanding of it. This statement is predicated upon the proposition that an educated or cultured person is one who through study, discipline, training, and experience has developed the capacity to understand and interpret the things which he encounters in life. The more highly one develops this capacity the greater is one's culture.

Knowledge of every kind adds to understanding and therefore has cultural value. The extent of this value depends upon the nature of the knowledge. In general, the more highly specialized knowledge is, the less its cultural value. For this reason the cultural value of technical studies is relatively low while that of studies in the humanities is relatively high.

Technical studies are narrow and restricted. Their primary purpose is the extension of the control of man over things. Social studies are broad and general. Their primary purpose is to gain an understanding of the effects which the extension of control over things has had and will have upon society as a whole. Or, when human activities are viewed as a unity, it can be said that those engaged in technical studies are interested in the mastery of parts, whereas those engaged in social studies are concerned with the understanding of the whole.

The distinction between technical and social studies is not wholly a matter of differences between the subjects to which they relate. It may be a matter of purpose. On the one hand, for those who intend to practice law, law is a technical study. Law students must place emphasis upon the mastery of parts. For them, cultural values are in the nature of by-products. On the other hand, for those interested primarily in the social significance of the law, it is a social study. Their emphasis is upon the whole. What they learn about the parts is little more than descriptive. This study is directed toward the latter group. Its emphasis is upon general understanding.

THE ALL-PERVADING IMPORTANCE
OF THE LAW

Relationships between persons, and relationships between persons and things, constitute the subject matter of the law; there is no relationship of either kind that does not come within its purview. There is nothing it does not command, prohibit, or permit. In its overall aspects the law—with the possible exception of history—is the broadest of social studies, and, apart from the description of wars, history is in large part but the story of the rise and fall of legal institutions. The story of the peoples who were subjected to the rule of Rome, the narrative of life in England under the feudal system, and the division of American history into periods—on the basis of the legal system under which the peoples who have occupied the territories of America have lived—bear witness to this. And what is current history and what will the history of this era be other than the story of the struggle between the conflicting ideologies that find their expression in the laws of the opposing powers?

The all-pervading importance of the law is further evidenced by the extent to which it enters into other studies. A sociologist must have some knowledge of the law, more especially criminal law, the law of torts, and the law of domestic relations. An economist cannot adequately explain the unlimited liability of partners without understanding the law of agency, the limited liability of the stockholders of a corporation without understanding what a person is in the eyes of the law, the nature of money, checks, promissory notes, and other bills of exchange without being able to distinguish between assignment and negotiation, or the production and distribution of goods and services under free enterprise without some acquaintance with private property and contract. And no citizen of the United States can understand, appreciate, and explain the privileges he enjoys, as compared with the citizens of some other countries, apart from a general understanding of the nature, need for, origin, and broad principles of the law of the society of which he is a part.

BASIC UNITY OF THE LAW

The use of such terms as engineering law, agricultural law, aviation law, business law, the law of medicine, and the law of real estate tends to create the impression that there is a division of law corresponding to each calling or profession. This is an error; there are but two distinct divisions of law: (1) *substantive law* which defines rights and duties and (2) *adjective law*, or the *law of procedure*, which provides for the enforcement of rights or the performance of duties and the punishment of wrongs.

The law of procedure is divided into rules governing the conduct of criminal and civil actions. Substantive law is divided into the law of contract, the law of torts, and criminal law. Division beyond this, that is, division into fields, apart from statutes of limited application, involves nothing more than the application of the rules of substantive law to particular situations. They are based upon the things and the relationships to which the principles of the law are applied and not upon variations in legal principles. Apart from statutes relating to specific activities there is but one law to which all persons, regardless of their occupations or callings, are subject. It is more meaningful, therefore, to speak of the law as applied in a particular field than of the law of that field. This is easily illustrated.

Due care in keeping a pathway in safe condition is something different from due care in filling a prescription. Nonetheless, the liability of a pharmacist to a person injured as the result of his carelessness in filling a prescription is the same as that of a person in possession of a house, who, because of failure to sand an icy approach, causes another person to be injured by a fall. The basic principle or rule applicable in both cases is that every person in every relationship is obligated to exercise reasonable care for the safety of other persons. Failure to do so is the essence of the tort of negligence. The rule is everywhere the same. It is only the situations to which, and the circumstances under which, it is applied that differ.

Not every careless act that results in injury is a tort. Therefore, to determine whether or not a person charged with negligence is liable, one must know first what makes an act a tort and, second, what degree of care has been held to be reasonable under similar circumstances. The first involves the elements common to all torts and the second the decisions which have been handed down by the courts in like cases. Thus it is that the law of torts in general, plus the rules of negligence in particular, plus the decisions in pharmaceutical cases, is thought of in terms of pharmaceutical law; while the same law of torts, plus the same rules of negligence, plus the decisions of the courts in real estate cases is thought of as part of the law of real estate. And so it is throughout the field of human activities. What is true with respect to negligence and other torts is true also with respect to the law in general. This is apparent everywhere but nowhere more so than in the field of real estate.

COMPONENTS OF THE LAW OF REAL ESTATE

Title to real estate may be held by an individual, by an association of individuals, by a corporation, or by a trust. It may be held severally, jointly, in common, or in community. The laws governing these relationships differ. Take taxation for example. To decide how the title to any given piece or parcel of realty should be held, it is necessary to be acquainted with all the forms of ownership organization, to be familiar with the various types of tenancy, and to understand the creation and operation of trusts.

The legal rights which may attach to real estate are many and varied. One who holds it subject only to the superior rights of the state and the law of tort, holds it in fee simple. He who, as owner, mortgages real estate as security for the repayment of a debt reduces his interest in it to what is called his equity of redemption. One who leases real estate to another retains a reversionary interest in it, while the party to whom it is leased gets a temporary estate. A person entitled to receive what is left of an estate, after the claims of another person have been satisfied, owns what is known as a remainder. One who has the right, as opposed to permission, which is described as license, to go upon the land or realty of another for his own purposes enjoys an easement. This listing is not meant to be complete; however, it should serve to illustrate the complexity of the property rights with which the law of real estate deals.

Interests in real estate are transferred in many and diverse ways. Outright sales, the sale of easements, and the granting of leases are matters of contract. Most contracts involving interests in real estate fall within the statute of frauds. Hence, they must be formally drawn. Transfer of title consequent upon the execution of judgments and foreclosure proceedings are in the nature of forced sales. The establishment of title through adverse possession, the perfecting of easements through use, the creation of prescriptive rights in the case of nuisances, the reversion of title to the state through escheat and the disposal of the property of one who dies intestate result from the operation of law. All of these, as well as transfers effected through gifts between the living and those resulting from the execution of a will, come within the province of real estate law.

In financing real estate transactions, individuals, banks, and other financial institutions use, in addition to cash, many kinds of financial instruments and follow many methods. The terms check, promissory note, negotiable, nonnegotiable, mortgage, mortgage bonds, collateral trust bonds, debentures, registered bonds, bearer bonds, etc., all have legal significance and all are used in connection with real estate.

Private property is held subject to the right of eminent domain, the police power, the power to tax, and the law of tort. Under eminent domain the state, upon giving just compensation, can take anything it needs for public use. Under the police power it can regulate the use of it, and, if need be, destroy property without giving compensation when the health, safety, or general welfare of the public demands it. Under the power to levy and collect taxes and special assessments it may have real estate sold to satisfy its claims if the owner fails to pay them, while under the law of tort the party in possession of realty not only owes certain duties to persons who come upon it, he may not use it in any way that will interfere with others in the reasonable enjoyment of their rights.

Real estate taxes and special assessments are levied on the property and not on the owner. Claims of the state take precedence over other claims. Thus all interests in real estate are bought and sold or otherwise transferred subject to the laws under which claims of the state arise. The person who buys real property upon which back taxes or special assessments are owing must pay them in order to retain his title.

One who goes upon the land of another without leave or license is a trespasser; one who has tacit permission to enter for his own benefit is a licensee; one who has permission and enters not only for his own benefit but also for that of the party in legal possession is an invitee. The duties owed by legal possessors of land to those who come upon it depends upon whether they are trespassers, licensees, or invitees.

Whether or not the occupier of land can be stopped from using it for a certain purpose on the ground that he is interfering with the right of another to enjoy his property, that is, whether or not a nuisance is being committed, depends in the first place upon such factors as location and time, and in the second place upon how long the occupier has been putting the land to such use, that is, upon whether or not he has established a prescriptive right.

Most failures on the part of one person to respect the rights of another are tortious, but some amount to crimes. And some are both torts *and* crimes. Forced entry upon realty by an unauthorized person is both a tort and a crime. Entry without leave or license is only trespassing. The mere maintenance of a nuisance is a tort. To maintain a nuisance in violation of a statute is both a tort and a crime. Therefore, the criteria by which torts are distinguished from crimes, together with eminent domain, the police power, the power to tax and levy special assessments, the rules of negligence, the rules of nuisance and many other matters either mentioned or to be mentioned, are part of the law of real estate. And, inasmuch as one should know what to do when a tort or a crime has been committed, the occupier and/or the party entitled to the possession of realty should understand the rudiments of legal procedure.

We could pursue this line of thought until we had covered the gamut of the law, but to do so would be pointless. More than enough has been said to substantiate the statement that it is one thing to speak of or recognize a field of law and quite another to delineate its boundaries. This delineation is difficult because the legal framework of society is basically a unit in the sense that it is made up of related parts. This statement epitomizes much of what we have said, but, inasmuch as its meaning may be none too clear, we seek to clarify it through analogy.

AN ANALOGY

Subject to the limitations inherent in analogy, the legal institutions of a society may be likened to the skeleton of an animal or the framework of a plant, more especially to that of a tree. Just as the cores of the branches that grow from the trunk of a tree are composed of the same substance as the core of the trunk, so the cores of specially designated branches of substantive law are but the extensions of the principles which make up the main body of the law. And just as the trunk, branches, and twigs of a tree support its living bark, foliage, flowers, and fruit, so the laws of a society support the institutions through which it lives, grows, and yields its fruit, whether they be of tyranny or freedom.

A skeleton or framework is something more than the parts of which it is composed. To comprehend the purpose and significance of any bone in the skeleton of a mammal, or of any fiber in the framework of a plant, it is necessary to be acquainted in some measure with the whole. And in order to comprehend the importance of any part or division of any legal structure enough must be known about the structure to view the part or division in its relationship to the whole. To hold that one can gain an adequate understanding of any section of law, in any legal system, by studying it in isolation is to ignore the effect it has on other sections and the effects which other sections have upon it. It is akin to holding that one can come to comprehend a tree through the contemplation of a twig.

A tree, by adding new wood here and discarding old wood there, changes its frame to meet its changing needs. A young tree produces low branches which wither and die as the tree pushes upward through the forest. A society is a changing organism. Many laws suitable to a young society are not suitable to a mature one. Hence a healthy, progressive society is always adding a new law here and discarding an old law there to make and to keep the framework of its institutions strong.

Dead, low branches protruding from the trunk of a tree serve only to entangle and impede the progress of those who wish to pass through a forest. Outdated and outmoded laws, protruding as it were from the trunk of the law, serve only to confuse and retard the progress of those who must find their way along them. The dead branches of a tree, and others that serve no useful purpose, should be pruned; and laws that lend no aid to social progress should, depending upon their nature, be either modified by the courts or repealed through legislation.

THE MATTER OF PURPOSE

Thus far it has not been our intention to instruct. This chapter has fulfilled its purpose if it has awakened interest in, and has demonstrated the need on the part of the American people for, some basic legal understanding. In it, to show the scope, the social significance, and the underlying unity of American law, we have made particular mention of many legal matters. Few, if any of these, will be mentioned again in this study and none will be explained. This is in keeping with our general or overall objective, which is not to teach the law as such but rather to awaken what we may call legal awareness on the part of all and to lay a background which will enable those who elect to study law:

1. To view it in its relationships;
2. To more easily comprehend and integrate its parts (much as the outline and coloring of the picture to be constructed aid one in assembling a jig-saw puzzle); and
3. To appreciate or come to an appreciation of the great responsibility which the legal profession imposes, or should impose, upon those who engage in it.

Chapter 2

PHYSICAL AND

MORAL LAW

DISTINCTION BETWEEN BASIC AND
POLITICAL LAW

A generic term causes the mind to select, from the many things to which it may refer, the thing with which it is most familiar. Law is a generic term. Hence it usually calls to mind the law that is personified by public officials. This law has been defined in many ways but for us it is best described as a pattern of conduct which a politically organized society stands ready to impose by force upon those members who would not of their own volition conform with it. It is man-made, and is known both as secular and as political law. It is the law referred to in the phrase—so dear to Americans—"liberty under law." It is the law to which this study as a whole relates, but it is not law in the sense in which the term is used in connection with the subject matter of this chapter, namely, the operation of basic laws in the realms of the physical and metaphysical, the dependence of man-made political law upon metaphysical laws, and the relationship between man-made laws and liberty.

A CONCEPT OF LIBERTY: LIBERTY
WITHIN THE LAW

If liberty is, as we define it, the right of the individual to act in accordance with his own beliefs, that is, freedom to do as he pleases, then "liberty" under man-made law is a myth. This must be true if political law is a pattern of conduct which a politically organized society stands ready to impose by force upon its members. Liberty is not simply a matter of belief; it includes freedom to act in accordance with belief. It is not something that can be imposed upon men from without; it is something that arises from within them. Man-made law does not create liberty, it curtails it. Hence "liberty within the law" expresses the American ideal better than "liberty under law."

When the automobile was invented, motorists were free to drive, within the capacity of their machines, at speeds of their own choosing. They were subject only to the rules of negligence. Today, maximum speed limits are the rule, and on superhighways minimum as well as maximum speeds are set. Where the minimum speed is forty miles per hour and the maximum is sixty-five miles, the freedom of a motorist to vary his pace is bounded by these limits. This illustrates what we mean by freedom within the law.

The backward peoples of the world are not to be "liberated" by imposing upon them the democratic form of government. It is only as they come to believe in democracy as a way of life that free democratic governments can be organized to function effectively within their territories. It is not in the nature of things that all men should hold the same beliefs.

PHYSICAL LAW

Generically, the term law connotes regularity, dependability, and order. Man, early in his history, came to recognize that the planets move regularly in their orbits; that he can depend upon the sun to rise and set, the tides to ebb and flow, the seasons to come and go at times definitely appointed. In time he came to reason that back of the order observed in these and other physical phenomena there must be controlling forces. He described these forces as laws, and, as he thought of the universe or nature wholly in terms of the physical, he came to speak of the laws of nature.

Paradoxical as it may seem, the laws of nature must be distinguished from natural law. As a matter of usage, the former relate to things physical while the latter refers to a philosophically speculative system of principles, independent of enacted laws which is thought to be innate in the nature of man. In keeping with this concept of natural law, and without attempting to define it, judges frequently speak of natural justice.

Parts or divisions of the laws of nature relating to specific fields of investigation constitute the laws of the separate sciences. The laws of physics and the laws of chemistry are good examples. Directly stated, a law of nature is the intangible factor which acts upon a given cause to bring about a predictable result. This involves the principle of probability.

THE PRINCIPLE OF PROBABILITY

Situations exist in which the result that will flow from a single circumstance or a single experiment cannot be accurately predicted, whereas the result that will flow from a set of similar circumstances or a series of like experiments can be. Thus an actuary cannot name the members of a group of ten thousand men, aged fifty, who will be living a year hence, but he can calculate with surprising accuracy the number that will die. If an experimenter throws ten coins into the air he cannot predict with accuracy the number of "heads" that will appear upon a single throw, but he can calculate quite accurately, on the basis of ten thousand throws, how often a given number of "heads" will appear. This is attributed to the operation of an intangible factor, which, owing to the consistency with which it works, is called the law of probability or the law of chance. Thus it is that man postulates in the physical realm what we here call a basic law wherever and whenever he can predict results with a reasonable degree of accuracy.

The recognition of basic laws depends upon the certainty with which certain results can be attributed to certain causes. Indeed, the importance of cause-and-effect relationships is such that the phrase "the law of cause and effect" is in common use. This, however, involves a misconception of basic law. A cause-and-effect relationship is not a law; it is, rather, the manifestation of the operation of a law. This is emphasized because cause-and-effect relationships are the criteria used later to establish that basic laws operate in the realm of the metaphysical as well as in the physical, and are, in fact, the chief factor in the control of human conduct.

METAPHYSICAL LAW

That there are natural physical laws is everywhere apparent. It is through his knowledeg of these laws that man controls his physical environment. That there are natural, metaphysical laws is not so apparent. Nonetheless, on the basis that creation is a unity, it is but reasonable to hold that there are metaphysical as well as physical laws, and that the operation of the one is provable in the same manner as the operation of the other.

Normal persons are so constituted that different mental states result from different types of conduct. Conduct in conformity with custom begets a feeling of satisfaction whereas conduct in conflict with custom has the opposite effect. Conduct in conformity with what one believes to be right begets a sense of justification whereas conduct in conflict with one's beliefs results in a sense of guilt.

Here are cause-and-effect relationships. Here are intangible control factors in operation. Here are metaphysical laws to be taken into consideration by all persons interested in the making and/or enforcement of political law. We call the first the law of custom and the second the moral law.

BELIEF-BEHAVIOR COMPLEX

The body of man is subject to physical laws, but man is more than flesh. He possesses the capacity to think. He can know happiness. He can feel remorse. These are mental states. Hence man was prompted at an early date to ask, as he still asks, "On what does the condition of the mind depend?" The answer is to be found, at least in part, in the relationship between belief and action, that is, in the belief-behavior complex.

THE MORAL LAW

The intangible control factor which causes men to feel justified when they do that which they believe to be right, and guilty when they do that which they believe to be wrong, is our concept of the moral law. It is an operative rather than a static thing, and is not to be confused with stated moral and ethical codes, such as the Ten Commandments. Codes of ethics change as society changes. The moral law is always and everywhere the same. It is always and everywhere the control factor that operates within the belief-behavior complex to create either a sense of justification or a sense of guilt in the minds of individuals. The relationship between belief and action or inaction is the cause upon which the moral law operates.

Absolute v. Relative Morality

Apart from the capacity to draw distinctions, there is no moral problem. All acts are amoral unless the actor is capable of making an intelligent choice. Capacity to choose, however, is not enough. Before one can choose between right and wrong one must hold beliefs with respect to what is right and what is wrong. This presents a fundamental question. From whence do these beliefs come? Are human acts innately right or wrong, moral or immoral? Is the sense of justification, associated with certain conduct, a preordained result of such conduct, or does man consider acts to be right or moral which advance what he believes to be his own good, and acts to be wrong and immoral which in his estimation have the opposite effect?

Men are not in agreement with respect to the origin of concepts of right and wrong. At one extreme there are those who believe right and wrong to be matters of Divine determination revealed to man. To these, morality is an absolute, not a relative, matter. They are moral absolutists. They think of the moral law as being in the metaphysical realm what natural law is in the physical realm. This is to say, they regard it as a control factor that acts upon preordained causes to bring about predetermined results. At the other extreme are those who think of beliefs in right and wrong as being relative to time and place. To these, the moral law is the control factor that acts upon mutable causes to bring about predictable results. These are moral relativists.

The difference between the above points of view is found not in the concept of the law involved but in the nature of the causes upon which the law operates. They are in conflict with respect to the origin of the criteria by which conduct is to be judged. They are in agreement with respect to the cause-and-effect relationship which exists between conduct and state of mind. This may be summarized thus: Those who consider right and wrong to be matters relative to time and place agree that the believer in revelation, who lives according to his beliefs, will experience a sense of justification as the result of so doing. And persons who believe in revelation may well agree that those who believe in the relativity of right and wrong and who act in accordance with their beliefs will also experience a sense of justification. But those who conceive of right and wrong in terms of absolutes cannot agree that the sense of justification experienced by those who conceive of them in relative terms is justified.

That men differ with respect to the origin of concepts of right and wrong is of little concern to those interested in the control of human conduct. What matters to them is that there is agreement with respect to the fundamental importance of what men believe.

RESPONSIBILITY FOR BELIEFS

The fact that beliefs are the result of either revelation or experience does not relieve man from all responsibility. It is the duty of each man, as an intelligent being, to ask, "What do I believe, from whence do my beliefs come, and upon what evidence are they based?"[1] As these and other similar questions are highly personal, only those who ask them can supply the answers. Therefore, that which follows immediately is presented merely as a point of departure; as a basis for discussion or as a working hypothesis.

---

[1] See p. 41, Duty to Question Beliefs; also p. 46, Freedom to Study Alternatives.

MORAL CRITERION

When it is granted, as we believe it must be granted if life is to have meaning, that there are purposes in nature, we have a basis upon which to distinguish right from wrong, good from evil, the moral from the immoral, and the amoral from each or all of these.

It is generally believed that man alone possesses the power of foresight, that only he has the ability to foresee the results of his acts. This is the basis upon which choices between lines of conduct are made. Hence no creature, apart from man, is confronted with a moral problem. The lower animals, when left to themselves, intuitively fulfill the purposes for which they are born. Therefore their acts are amoral. Man alone asks why he is here and seeks to discover the end or ends which nature has in view. This he does in order that he may mold his conduct in conformity with it or them. What then is the primary purpose of nature?

If man is, as he believes himself to be, the highest form of life, or the crowning creation for whose benefit all else has been brought into being—it matters not whether by a single act or through the process of evolution—the primary purpose of nature must be the promotion of human welfare. This must be the great good, and unless nature is a paradox (which concept we reject) her laws must be designed to promote it. They, therefore, are good. This must be what men mean when they speak of the universe as being moral. Herein lies a criterion by which to judge human conduct and herein we find the premise upon which we base the conclusion that when the beliefs of men are such as to lead them to act in keeping with the laws of nature their acts are right or moral in the absolute or ultimate sense, whereas acts in keeping with beliefs not in conformity with these laws are only relatively moral, that is, moral in relation to the beliefs.

BELIEFS, NOT CONDUCT, DETERMINE MENTAL RESPONSE

In every society there are certain mandates and certain taboos in the approved pattern of conduct. These vary between societies, yet a member of any society who believes in the pattern of conduct approved by it, and conforms thereto, will experience a mental response similar to that of a member of any other society who believes in and conforms to the pattern of conduct of which it approves. If he conforms he will feel justified. If he fails to conform he will experience a sense of guilt.

When the above cause-and-effect relationships are considered separately, neither appears to be open to question, but when they are compared it appears that like results have been derived from different causes. This is to say we find individuals who have followed different patterns of conduct experiencing the same metaphysical result, namely, a sense either of justification or remorse. It would appear that if unlike patterns of conduct effect like results, there is either more than one moral law operative or there is more than one cause which, under the operation of the moral law, will produce the same foreseeable result. Neither alternative is valid since a pattern of conduct, as such, is never the cause upon which the moral law operates. The cause is always the relationship which exists between the act or acts of the actor and his beliefs with respect to whether said acts are right or wrong.

The pagan who mortifies his flesh to sanctify his spirit, thereby gaining a sense of justification, is relatively as moral as the Christian who cares for his body in the manner his faith demands. This is not to call absolute morality, which we have acknowledged and defined, into question; it is but to emphasize that, in the control of conduct through the operation of the moral law, it is what men believe to be right and wrong and not what is right and wrong in the absolute sense that matters. That which is involved is relative, not absolute, morality. To reiterate: when the beliefs of a person are in keeping with the purposes of nature, and his acts are in keeping with his beliefs, the acts are absolutely moral; when the acts of a person are in keeping with his beliefs, but his beliefs are not in conformity with the purposes of nature, they are relatively moral. Because it is what man believes and not the validity of his beliefs, in terms of eternal verities, that controls his conduct, the quest for absolute morality is beyond the scope of this study. It falls within the field of religion.

To those who think in terms of absolutes, the concept of relative morality is heresy. But for those who wish to understand how conduct is conditioned by belief it is indispensable.

PHYSICAL DISTINGUISHED FROM METAPHYSICAL EFFECTS

When it is granted that there are purposes in nature, that these purposes are good, and that the laws of nature are designed to promote them, it follows that violation of these laws has moral implication. However, care must be exercised not to attribute the effects of the operation of physical laws to the operation of the moral law.

The use of some drugs is detrimental to the physical well-being of man. Our society believes man is under duty to care for his physical health. Hence, the taking of deleterious substances into his body is considered wrong, sinful, or immoral. However, the physical deterioration, including that of the brain and nervous system, that results from the use of these is not to be attributed to the operation of the moral law. A child too young to have moral responsibility would suffer from their use in the same way as a normal adult. It must be, therefore, that some law of nature, some physical law or law of health, is at work which says, in effect, that the taking of these substances into our bodies will eventually destroy them.

It is because we believe it to be wrong to destroy our bodies that we regard the use of things injurious to them as sinful. Prior to the holding of this belief, no moral issue could arise. This must be true since our beliefs are the causes upon which the moral law operates to create within us either a good or a bad conscience. It is the sense of remorse felt by the drug addict in his rational moments, and not the ravages of his mind and body, that are attributable to the operation of the moral law. An addict who really believed in the righteousness of his addiction would suffer no remorse.

METAPHYSICAL LAWS IN OPERATION

The intensity of the sense of justification which one experiences when one acts in conformity with one's beliefs, and the intensity of the sense of guilt one experiences when one acts otherwise, are proportional to the strength of the beliefs upon which the moral law operates. It is human to seek the pleasurable and avoid the painful. Thus it is natural for one to seek the sense of justification, which comes from doing that which one believes to be right. Or, speaking negatively, one naturally seeks to avoid the sense of guilt, which comes from doing that which one believes to be wrong. This is the belief-behavior complex. It is important to those interested in the control of human conduct because there is little need for man-made law in the case of persons who believe firmly enough in the pattern of conduct, approved by their society, that they, of their own volition, conduct themselves in conformity with it.

That which we have called the law of custom operates in much the same way as the moral law but the causes upon which it operates are different. Hence it produces different results. The moral law operates upon our beliefs with respect to what is right and what is wrong to create within us either a sense of justification or a sense of guilt. The law of custom operates on what we think is, or is not, socially acceptable, to create within us a feeling of self-satisfaction or self-dissatisfaction, depending upon whether or not our conduct is in keeping with the conduct of others.

When a normal person follows a pattern of conduct or a custom, and thereby gains social approval, he experiences a feeling of self-satisfaction but not a sense of justification. Conversely, when a normal person violates a custom, he, being mindful of the disapproval of others, experiences a feeling of self-dissatisfaction but not a sense of guilt. A timid youth who fails to tip his hat to a lady may well be greatly perturbed, but his state of mind differs greatly from that which would result from an act considered by him to be sinful. The feeling of self-dissatisfaction he would experience in the first instance would result from the operation of the law of custom. The feeling of guilt he would experience in the second instance would result from the operation of the moral law.

Just as the moral law places man under pressure to conduct himself in conformity with his beliefs, so the law of custom places him under pressure to conduct himself in conformity with the pattern approved and followed by others. These pressures may act in unison or in opposition.

One may believe a custom to be either moral or immoral. Thus a man who follows what he believes to be a moral custom may experience both a feeling of self-satisfaction and a sense of justification; he enjoys a dual reward. A man who follows what he believes to be an immoral custom may well have the feeling of self-satisfaction that he sought to gain more than offset by a sense of guilt. It is the all-but-universal pervasiveness of the moral issue that makes the moral law the most important factor in the control of conduct.

STYLES AND MANNERS

The operation of the law of custom is nowhere more apparent than in the field of fashion. For convenience we divide this field into two parts: fashion with respect to things or style, as in the case of clothes, and fashion with respect to conduct, which we call manners.

To many persons there are few things more depressing than being out of style. They want to have what others have and to do as others do. Such persons will go to almost any length to gain the self-satisfaction which they enjoy as the result of their conformity. This is so widely recognized and so generally understood that anything more than mere mention of it would be superfluous. There is, however, a great difference between the importance of styles in things and styles in conduct, known as manners; hence the statement, sometimes heard, that good manners are out of date should cause concern to all.

Manners are not merely matters of form; they are, in general, the outward manifestation of the inner attitude of the individual with respect to the rights of other individuals. Thus when allowance is made for those who, because of ignorance, are uncouth, and for those who use good manners to cover up nefarious designs, a good-mannered person may be said to be one who respects—in the sense that he tries not to violate—the rights of other persons and who expresses his appreciation to all persons who respect his rights. Conversely, an ill-mannered person is one who neither respects the rights of others nor expresses his appreciation to those who respect his rights. A person of good manners either asks to be excused or apologizes when, through accident or necessity, he violates the right of another person. An ill-mannered person, under like circumstances, does neither.

There is a direct correlation between manners and man-made law. This may be either positively or negatively expressed. Good manners decrease the need for law whereas bad manners increase it.

The decline in manners in the United States is to be viewed with apprehension. It is a symptom of decline in respect for the rights of others and is therefore a threat to the democratic way of life. It offers a challenge to the parents of the rising generation. It is up to them to teach good manners until they become a matter of habit on the part of their children. In so doing they will mitigate the necessity for man-made law and will strengthen the foundation of American freedom.

Chapter 3

LAW AND

CONDUCT

INADEQUACY OF METAPHYSICAL
CONTROL FACTORS

The laws of nature are the forces that rule and regulate the physical universe. Man is subject to these laws, but human living consists of more than the relationship between man and his physical environment; it involves membership in a social order. This is to say that it involves membership in an association of human beings in which order is achieved, *as order* can only be achieved, through the operation of law.

Control over the acts of man is essential to the existence of a human society, just as control over the planets and stars is essential to the existence of the universe. But whereas the control factors innate in nature have, in and of themselves, operated so as to maintain an orderly adjustment throughout physical creation, the control factors innate in man have failed, in and of themselves, to achieve a like result in the area of human relations. Hence the need for the external pressures man-made law provides.

In a way analogous to that in which natural law keeps the planets in their places and the stars on their courses, man-made rules have as their goal the establishment and maintenance of order among men. This is why they are called law. These rules, however, are not law in the sense in which the term is used in connection with physical creation or nature. Neither are they law in the sense in which the term is used with respect to the metaphysical, as in moral law.

A disregard of either natural or moral law brings its own punishment, but this is not true of man-made laws. With the latter, punishment must be consciously imposed. Expose yourself to the law of gravity and you fall. Act contrary to your moral precepts and you suffer pangs of conscience. Violate a man-made law without detection and, apart from any punishment the moral law imposes, you will go scot-free.

SOME AGENCIES OF SOCIAL CONTROL

Many institutions, or agencies of social control, make rules relating to human conduct. Among these are the home, fraternal organizations, labor unions, business and professional associations, the Church, and the State. Whether or not a man-made rule amounts to law depends upon whether or not the agency which made it has the right to compel the public in general to observe it. Rules, depending wholly on public opinion for enforcement, are not law.

In countries where there is an overlapping of Church and State, both Church and State have the right to use force in the field of secular affairs. Hence, rules made by the Church, as well as rules made by the State, are recognized as law. Rules made and enforceable by a State are political law. Rules made and enforceable by the Church are ecclesiastical law. In the United States, due to the separation of Church and State, government is the only agency authorized to use physical force. Therefore, in this country, only rules made by the government, or by some agency of government, are law.

ECCLESIASTICAL LAW

Ecclesiastical law was, and in countries where the separation of Church and State has not been fully effected still is, an independent body of law enforced by church (or ecclesiastical) courts. In its beginning, ecclesiastical law applied only to the clergy and to matters wholly ecclesiastical. In consequence, the jurisdiction of ecclesiastical courts, this is to say the right to hear and decide cases, was strictly limited. But as time advanced, ecclesiastical law was broadened and the jurisdiction of ecclesiastical courts correspondingly extended until the laity was brought largely, but never wholly, within its scope.

The extension of the jurisdiction of the church courts was based upon the proposition that it is the function of the Church to deal with sin, and sin was given a wide interpretation. Most offenses committed by the laity were triable under secular law in state or secular courts, but, in the event that they were not tried there, they could be tried by the church courts.

Such state or secular courts as existed in the Middle Ages were weak, and for the most part inaccessible. Thus, at the peak of their power, the ecclesiastical courts had all but complete jurisdiction over acts which are today classified as crimes. Nor did their jurisdiction stop there. On the grounds that promises are morally binding, they took jurisdiction over promise-breakers as sinners. The reasoning behind this was that a person to whom a promise is made has the moral right to act upon it in anticipation of its fulfillment, and if he, the promisee, does so, and suffers injury as the result of the failure of the promisor to perform, justice demands that the promisor be held accountable.

The application of this principle of good faith, of fairness or equity by the church courts, marks the beginning of the law of contract; it was, one might say, the seedling which when transplanted via equity into the field of law, developed into the legal institution of contract. The story of this and other contributions of the ecclesiastical courts to equity and law, though interesting, is too long and too complicated to be recited here.

One reason for the wide jurisdiction of ecclesiastical courts was that no organization existed that was powerful enough to challenge the authority of the Church. But with the development of strong national governments, the situation changed. This resulted in a struggle for domination between Church and State. In this struggle the Church has come off second best. Its jurisdiction over temporal affairs, especially in non-Roman Catholic countries, has been greatly curtailed. In England, where some vestiges of the oneness of Church and State remain, ecclesiastical courts still possess, in theory at least, the right to adjudicate and punish immoral acts. In practice, however, they try such offenses only when they are committed by members of the clergy of the Church of England.

In the United States, there are neither ecclesiastical courts nor ecclesiastical law in the English sense, although churches may, and do, make rules and regulations for the guidance of their clergies and their members. They may and do create bodies to hear and decide matters pertaining to church organization and discipline. But such bodies are not courts in the legal sense. Their jurisdiction rests on a consensual basis. They cannot compel parties alleged to be at fault to appear before them. They cannot subpoena witnesses. They cannot cite recalcitrant witnesses for contempt. They do not have the right to imprison or to impose physical punishment upon those who ignore their decrees.

The story of the struggle between Church and State over

temporal power is, in brief, as follows. The Church held that those who failed to follow its moral teaching sinned, and that its function was (as it still is) to deal with sin. The State held that it is one thing to deal with sin as such, but quite another to deal with the physical consequences of sin. The right of the Church to deal with the former was not questioned, but that it had the right to deal with the latter was vigorously denied. Temporal matters, said the adherents of the State, are matters with which the State or secular courts should deal. In essence, the issue resolved itself to this: Which organization, the Church or the State, should supplement the moral law by providing physical punishment for wrongful acts?

Regardless of who makes the rules providing for the infliction of physical punishment, they are made to dissuade persons, who would not be restrained by conscience, from doing that which their society considers wrongful. The underlying theory is that fear of physical punishment in the present is a greater deterrent to wrongful action than either the promise of reward for virtue or the threat of torment of spirit in a world to come.

SECULAR, POLITICAL, OR MAN-MADE LAW

The relationship between ethical or moral codes and man-made law is such that it is at times difficult to determine whether or not moral impulses should be supplemented by man-made law. In considering this problem, the basic difference between metaphysical and physical control factors must be kept in mind. This difference is that whereas metaphysical control factors (of which the moral law is the most important) operate through the medium of inner sanctions, physical control factors must rely upon the application of external pressures. Hence, that which cannot be controlled through the use of physical force should not be made the subject of man-made law.

Man-made laws give man the choice of acting in certain ways, or of suffering man-made consequences. It is with acts, not thoughts, that these laws deal. A person may think any thoughts he likes with impunity, as far as man-made laws are concerned; it is only when he expresses them, or reveals them through overt acts, that man-made law can take cognizance of them. Thus it is that the Judeo-Christian code of ethics, as it relates to acts, has been largely incorporated into law in the Western world whereas, insofar as it relates to metaphysical matters, it has not been so incorporated. An analysis of the Ten Commandments makes this clear. External pressures can be applied to induce conformity with the Commandment "Thou shalt not kill," but the Commandment "Thou shalt not covet" depends for its fulfillment upon the still, small voice of conscience.

Secular or political law, hereafter referred to simply as the law, consists of man-made rules relating to temporal affairs. It has to do with the relationship of men one with another, and with the relationship between men and things, as contrasted with spiritual matters which are the concern of the Church.

The rules of the law fall into three groups:

1. Those which relate to the amoral; i.e., matters with respect to which no question of right or wrong arises;
2. Those the purpose of which is to supplement metaphysical control factors, more especially the moral law; and
3. Those which specify the procedures to be followed in the matter of law enforcement.

Groups one and two consist of the rules that state and define the rights and duties recognized by the law. These are the substance of the law, for which reason they are called substantive law. Group three sets forth the ways in which the rights recognized and defined by substantive law can be enforced, or the procedure through which a person who owes a duty can be held liable for its nonperformance. In other words, group three consists of the law of procedure or remedial law (sometimes referred to as adjective law. This is because it does not stand alone but goes along with substantive law in a way analogous to that in which an adjective goes along with a noun). Procedural law provides for the enforcement of substantive law. Apart from substantive law the term procedural law has no meaning.

Many people think evils can be corrected through the mere passing of laws. Nothing could be farther from the truth. It is not as much in the making of just laws as it is in their enforcement that justice is achieved. A right without an effective remedy availeth nothing; therefore the gravest of responsibilities rests upon those charged with the administration of the law.

PROCEDURAL WEAKNESSES

American substantive law—apart from the overabundance of it, which is due no doubt to the blind belief of the people that it is a cure-all—is open to little adverse criticism. But American procedural law leaves much to be desired. It costs too much to go to law; justice for the poor and justice in small matters have been priced out of the courts. The courts are overburdened; it takes too long to get a final judgment. The belief in justice of too many lawyers is not strong enough to cause them to put the attainment of it above the winning of a case.

LAWS RELATING TO AMORAL MATTERS

When traffic developed to the extent that safety on the

highways could no longer be left to custom, courtesy, and good manners, the need for traffic laws arose. In other words, the need for traffic laws stems primarily from the fact that there are persons who do not believe sincerely enough in the rights of other persons to drive with care. The question as to which side of the road the driver of an automobile should use in passing another automobile, or which way he should turn when meeting one, involves no moral issue. In England the rule is to the left when meeting, to the right when passing. In the United States it is to the right when meeting, to the left when passing. The end sought—safety on the highways—is served as well by one set of rules as by the other. The vital point is that all who use the highways act in the same way; neither the choice of the English (to turn left) nor the choice of the Americans (to turn right) has moral significance.

However, once these choices were made and rules reflecting them had been promulgated, the social good of the respective societies required they be obeyed. Thus those to whom they applied were placed under a moral as well as a legal duty to observe them. The moral duty is the more significant. Reduction in the number of highway accidents depends primarily upon bringing those who use the highways to recognize their duties to others to the extent that they will voluntarily discharge them. Traffic laws are, at best, but mitigating measures.

To stress that the foregoing applies to all amoral matters, we will consider weights and measures. Our government sets the weight of the pound, the length of the foot, the content of the gallon, etc., and provides for the punishment of those who do not give legal weight and measure. Nonetheless, few will deny that whether or not a buyer gets what he bargains for depends largely upon the beliefs of the person who does the measuring or operates the scales.

LAWS RELATING TO MORAL MATTERS

Our laws are but the reflection of our beliefs. Before a right is recognized by the law it must be established as a matter of belief. We believe the promotion of human welfare involves the recognition of individual worth and the use—as opposed to the abuse—of private property. And, inasmuch as the promotion of human welfare is the criterion by which we judge morality, we, as a society, believe that voluntary, intentional acts that result in injury to the person or property of another are wrong and/or immoral. This is why persons and property are given legal protection. Man-made laws are necessary only when beliefs are not strongly or widely enough held to motivate conformity with them to the degree that we, as a society, deem desirable.

Because there are those among us who will not voluntarily respect what we, as a group, recognize to be the personal and property rights of others, we have the man-made law of torts; because there are those who do not always agree with respect to promises given and received, or, though agreeing, are reluctant to fulfill them, we have the man-made law of contracts; because there are those who are not restrained by conscience from acts deemed to be injurious to society, we have the man-made law of crime.

MORALS AND GOVERNMENT

We have defined man-made law as a pattern of conduct which a politically organized society stands ready to impose by force upon its members. Such patterns of conduct cannot be imposed indefinitely. In the last analysis, the stability of governments depends upon the beliefs of the governed. Dictators are aware of this, and, endeavoring to make the systems they have established endure, each strives to bring about a situation in which all persons subject to his rule will come to believe in the principles of his dictatorship. To achieve this, dictators employ two means: propaganda and elimination. Adults are propagandized, and those who prove susceptible and change their beliefs are welcomed into the dictatorial fold, while those who prove insusceptible are eliminated. Education is made a state monopoly and schools are converted into propaganda centers in which the children are taught to believe only that which the dictator wants them to believe. The end sought is clearly the control of conduct through the operation of the moral law. Propaganda of any kind succeeds only insofar as it influences conduct through its effect upon beliefs.

Just as a dictatorship cannot long endure unless those subject to it can be brought to believe in the principles upon which it is based, a democracy cannot continue indefinitely unless those who live under it believe sincerely enough in the principles of democracy to acquit themselves in the manner which the democratic way of life demands. This way of life is but the pattern of conduct which the moral law imposes upon those who sincerely believe in the rights of man as an individual. It is axiomatic that individuals can be allowed freedom to act only insofar as they can be trusted to act in ways which are not inimical to the social good.

The relationship between the moral law and political democracy was well understood by the framers of the Constitution of the United States. Benjamin Franklin, in a message to the Constitutional Convention at Philadelphia on September 17, 1789, said:

Sir, I agree to this Constitution with all its faults, if they are such, because I think a general Government necessary for us, and there is no form of government but what may be a blessing to the people if well administered, and I believe further, that this is likely to be well administered for a course of years, and can only end in despotism, as others have done before it, when the people shall become so corrupted as to need despotic government, being incapable of any other.

Those persons, and there are many in the United States, who deplore the encroachment of law on liberty through the extension of governmental control can find much food for thought here.

GOVERNMENTAL CONTROLS

It may be that the growth of governmental controls in the United States during the past few decades evidences, in some degree, the decline in morals which Benjamin Franklin foresaw. Or it may be that moral growth has not kept pace with material progress. Opinions may well differ as to whether or not our ancestors, on the whole, were more moral or less moral than we. It seems, however, that the inner controls to which they were subject, in relation to the temptations they had to face, were more adequate than our inner controls in relation to the temptations that confront us; and this is what matters.

To say that we are as moral as our fathers merely begs the question. It is the adequacy of our morality, not the relative degree, that is important; and that moral controls in many areas of human relationships are less adequate in the present than in the past seems everywhere apparent. Apart from this inadequacy there would be little or no need for much of our legislation. What is said here is well epitomized in the words: "There is no law against it." This means no man-made law. Hence, the implication is that the act referred to can be done with impunity. This is contrary to the whole tenor of our argument and is, as we have sought to show, the very antithesis of the principle upon which a free society must be based. To do that which society believes to be against its best interest, though legally allowable, is but to invite the enactment of more laws.

Because there are those who, to further their own economic interests, are willing to jeopardize the health and even the lives of other people, we have pure food and drug laws. Because there are those who do not believe sufficiently in the right of every man to a fair deal, we have fair trade and minimum wage laws. Because there are those who think only in terms of the present, we have resource conservation laws. In normal times we find it necessary to have many permanent commissions to supervise our activities; in emergencies we are forced to resort to temporary, but more rigid, controls. The Interstate Commerce Commission, the Securities Exchange Commission, and state public utilities commissions are examples of the former. Wartime price fixing and rent controls are examples of the latter.

The fact that business is regulated does not mean that all or most of those engaged in directing it are unmindful of their duties to society. We prefer to believe otherwise, and to cite the activities of such private organizations as Chambers of Commerce and Better Business Bureaus as substantiating this belief. That businessmen have been the first to have their activities publicly regulated is due to the importance of their services to society, and to the fact that the beliefs of the honest many among them have not been strong enough to cause them voluntarily to discipline the dishonest few—if this is possible in our society.

CONDUCT THAT INVITES CONTROLS

As our society becomes more complex, the problem of controls becomes greater. Consequently, there is little reason to hope, and still less reason to think (apart from a change in prevailing beliefs), that the march toward the regimentation of our lives will be checked.

Those who abuse the protection afforded by the Fifth Amendment to the Constitution of the United States are preparing the way for its abridgment. Legislators who forget that legislative immunity is granted to promote the free discussion of public business, and not as a shield behind which to commit character assassination, will have themselves to blame if it is curtailed. Surgeons who perform unnecessary operations on the ground that if they do not, others will, promote the socialization of medicine. Authors who write obscene books to command a market are asking for censorship. Craft unions that accept unqualified workmen into membership may find those who employ them will come to demand public certification of their skills. Manufacturers are now required to produce goods of approved quality. Laborers who combine demands for higher wages with restriction of output may cause the enactment of laws that require a minimum output. Employers are required to pay a minimum wage. Already the Supreme Court of the United States has upheld the right of the railroad industry to eliminate feather-bedding.

The list of those who through active abuse openly invite governmental regulation could be indefinitely extended. But they are not alone at fault; those who condone rather than condemn antisocial acts must also share the blame. Educators who substitute policy for principle will have little reason to complain if some day they are told what to teach. Clergymen who interpret the Scriptures in a way intended to soothe the consciences and increase the pledges of their parishioners are contributing nothing to strengthening—if indeed they are not undermining—the moral fiber of the nation. Church elders who pray over the Sacra-

ment on Sunday, and on Monday put nothing that cannot
be traced in their income tax returns; lawyers who use procedural technicalities to make a mockery of substantive law;
parents who think it clever, and thereby encourage their
children to smuggle themselves into places of amusement;
consultants who, upon learning the potential of a business,
organize a competitive concern; college professors and
others who, when invited to discuss matters of great public
interest, refrain from telling the whole truth as they know
it in order to avoid criticism and gain popularity; and others
of like ilk may be as high-principled as were their own ancestors, but only those who believe that practices of the
types here enumerated contribute to the social good can
argue honestly that those who engage in them are contributing to the growth of character, individual and national,
which must accompany the growing complexity of our social order if the greater temptations to which this growth
gives rise are to be voluntarily overcome. Are there such
persons?

DUTY TO QUESTION BELIEFS[1]

Conduct which gives rise to the need for man-made law,
judged on the basis of relative morality, does not indict for
immorality. The relative morality or immorality of individuals does not depend upon their conduct; it depends
upon the relationship between their beliefs and their conduct. Insofar as the individual is concerned, acts which conform with his beliefs are relatively moral and those that do
not conform are relatively immoral. It is axiomatic, however, that only conduct in conformity with honestly held
beliefs can meet the test of relative morality. This is to say

---

[1] See p. 20, Responsibility for Beliefs; also p. 46, Freedom to Study Alternatives.

that man is under a duty to question his beliefs. Can a person capable of making a rational choice, which is the criterion used in determining whether or not he is morally responsible, honestly believe that activities are to be adjudged as either right or wrong on the basis of the percentage of the population that engages in them? Would murder be justified if everyone claimed the right to kill? Would dishonesty become a virtue if everyone practiced it? Would rape be right if it became rampant? For all who believe the effect of an act on human welfare is the test of its morality, the answer to these and other questions of their kind is no.

PROGRESS AND THE MORAL LAW

As human welfare is best served through progress, namely the releasing of the body of man from overburdening toil and the liberation of his mind from blighting superstitions, the duty of questioning beliefs is self-apparent. Only those who examine their beliefs change them, and only through changes in beliefs is progress achieved.

It is through the evaluation of the results of his acts that man determines the validity of his beliefs, and it is through the exercise of his capacity to choose, and act on his choice, that he molds his conduct to further the purposes in which he believes. As tangible results are easier to evaluate than intangible results, the beliefs which underlie the techniques of physical production are more easily changed than beliefs evaluated in terms of their metaphysical results. Yet there are societies in the world, and groups within other societies, that so venerate the past as to attach moral significance to the productive processes employed by their fathers. To adopt new methods is sinful to them; hence, they refuse to alter the pattern of their ways. (In fact there are sects in the United States living today as they had lived in the horse and buggy days.) Indeed, the veneration of old ways is a factor which those charged with the administration of foreign aid must take into account when dealing with primitive, economically backward peoples. To adopt modern methods is sinful to them. The moral issue is so pervasive it cannot be disregarded in the consideration of any human problem.

BELIEFS AND LAW ENFORCEMENT

In areas in which the question of morality is directly presented, the law reflects the moral or ethical beliefs of those who make it. In a political democracy this is a majority of those interested enough in law making to cast their ballots. But this is not all. The enforceability of a law depends upon the extent and intensity of the belief of the people in the principle it is designed to uphold. To be enforceable a law must be in keeping with the prevailing beliefs of the people.[2]

The matter of law enforcement and/or the maintenance of the peace is not the concern of law enforcement officers only; and it is not enough that citizens as individuals obey the law, they must be willing to act to see that others obey it also. Indeed, the efficiency with which law is enforced depends upon the extent to which members of the public feel under moral compulsion

1. To report to the proper authorities those whom they know to be law-breakers;
2. To serve on juries;
3. To appear as witnesses; and
4. To assist the courts and/or all persons entrusted with the enforcement of the law in all other possible ways.

---

2 See p. 72, Law and Social Reform.

That the responsibility for effective law enforcement rests with the people as a whole is something which is not sufficiently understood, despite the importance of such understanding. Some idea of the fear and insecurity that would characterize life in the United States if all Americans came to believe that the safety of others is of no concern to them (in that the state employs police to maintain law and order), is to be gained from an examination of the facts in the Genovese murder case.[3]

On the night of March 13, 1964, a Miss Genovese, on her way home from work in one of the better neighborhoods of New York City, was stalked, and stabbed to death. Her death did not come quickly. Twice during a period of half an hour, her killer, apparently apprehensive that one of the onlookers would intervene, was frightened off. And twice, seeming to sense that no one intended to molest him, he returned to the attack. As was later disclosed, at least 37 persons heard the screams of Miss Genovese, and some of them witnessed one or more of the attacks. All 37 stood idly by while, to their certain knowledge, a crime which turned out to be murder was being committed in their vicinity. Not one of them attempted a rescue, which in view of the fact that the assailant twice fled in fright, could have been easily effected. Not one of them ventured to call the police, although it is evident that at least one of them believed that this should be done. Indeed this person at last summoned courage to leave his own apartment, from which he apparently had witnessed the crime, to go to the apartment of an elderly friend in a building presumably so situated that she could have had no personal knowledge of what was happening, to ask her to telephone the police. This she did, but her call was made too late.

---

[3] *New York Times*, March 27, 1964; also see Appendix.

We leave it to the criminologists and the social psychologists to explain the causes that give rise to the beliefs that in turn give rise to, or permit, antisocial conduct. We must content ourselves with the observation that, while pleas for more policemen and more police authority to cope with increasing crime are not to be ignored, the most effective crime deterrent is neither the number of police officers nor the extent of their authority; it is the active participation of the public in law enforcement. Had the man who ultimately went to his elderly friend and asked her to call the police had the courage to call them himself, when he first came to realize what was going on, a life might well have been saved. We do not claim fully to understand how courage is related to belief, but we are certain of the following: the men and women in the armed forces are not the only ones who must be brave if the United States is to remain the Land of the Free.

The Eighteenth Amendment to the Constitution of the United States was unenforceable because there were not enough people who believed in it firmly enough to cause them to assist those charged with the duty of enforcing it. There are few people in the United States who would not report a person whom they believed to be guilty of murder or arson, but there are many who did not, and there are many who would not, report illicit liquor sales, lest by so doing they would come to be known as informers.

CHANGES IN BELIEFS EFFECT CHANGES IN THE LAW

Changes in beliefs bring changes in the way men live, and thus make changes in the law necessary. For this reason, law making is an evolutionary process. Laws that reflect the beliefs of today, and are therefore enforceable, may well become, because of changed beliefs, unenforceable tomorrow, whereas laws that would be unenforceable today may well be enforceable tomorrow.

FREEDOM TO STUDY ALTERNATIVES[4]

A belief may be either ignorantly or intelligently held. Intelligently means the holder has considered the alternatives, and to do this he must be acquainted with them. He must be free to investigate. This is of paramount importance in the conflict between the East and the West. Russians who fear the effect on the Russian people of contacts with the Western world, and Americans who would deny to the American people the right to read about and evaluate communism, are alike in that they lack faith in the systems they advocate.

Ignorance is not the foundation upon which to build an enduring social order. Battles between ideologies are not won or lost through the suppression of truth. Neither are they resolved through the making of treaties. Their outcome depends upon what is in the hearts and minds of men. If freedom, as we know it, is not to enter another eclipse, those who enjoy it must not only believe in it to the point of great sacrifice, even life itself, they must, through teaching and example, lead others to do likewise. Mere lip service is not enough. It is not what men profess to believe but what they believe in fact that controls their conduct.

---

[4] See p. 20, Responsibility for Beliefs; also p. 41, Duty to Question Beliefs.

Chapter 4

LAW AND

GOVERNMENT

NATURE AND SEAT OF SOVEREIGNTY

Every creation is the manifestation of the exercise of some power. The law is a creation, and the power exercised in the creation of it is called sovereignty. Hence, some understanding of sovereignty is basic to an understanding of the law.

The law is a social phenomenon. Apart from a group or society of persons, there can be no law in the sense in which we have defined it, namely, as a pattern of conduct which a society stands ready to impose upon its members. Because law is a social phenomenon, sovereignty, or the power to make and enforce law, belongs to a society as a whole rather than to any individual or clique within it. A society possessed of sovereign power is a sovereign state.

A sovereign society exercises its powers through the instrumentality of government, or, differently stated, a government is the agency through which a sovereign society exercises its sovereign will in all matters other than the formation of its government. Thus, as a matter of definition, in the conduct of governmental affairs the people of a sovereign state are the principal; the government the agent.

An agent is a person who acts for and in the stead of a principal, in the exercise of powers which the principal expressly or impliedly grants. These are the only powers an agent may exercise, and it is the essence of agency that, in exercising them, an agent binds the principal. In the eyes of the law, the acts of the agent are the acts of the principal. Hence it is axiomatic that one person cannot become the agent of another person without such person's consent.

These are basic principles, which, when applied to governments, can mean only that when governments recognize each other as sovereign each tacitly acknowledges the other to be authorized by the people it governs to act as their agent; that is, each acknowledges that it regards the other as existing by the will of those being governed. If this is not true, in the contemplation of international law the practice of sovereign states in extending recognition to each other is no more than an empty gesture.[1] It is the recognition of its sovereignty by other sovereign states that brings an organized society into the family of sovereign states. But there is no rule which specifies the extent of the recognition required. The best we can say is that it need not be unanimous.

To be recognized as existing by the will of the governed a government need not be created directly by the people, as in democratic countries; it may be organized by a dynamic leader, as in Hitler's Germany, or it may be one which the masses passively tolerate, as some believe to be true in Russia.

That many societies throughout history have allowed an individual, or succession of individuals, to usurp and exercise sovereign power does not negate the proposition that governments exist by the will of the governed. In some instances it has taken peoples centuries to regain the political power lost by them when they either voluntarily made someone their ruler or permitted someone to establish himself as ruler over them.

---

[1] See p. 51, The Right of Governments to Bind the Governed.

It was the concentration of sovereign power in the person of Louis XIV of France that led him to say: "The State! I am the State!" whereas it was the sovereignty of the people reasserting itself in the French Revolution that demonstrated to Louis XVI, in a manner he could not well mistake, that in the last analysis, in monarchies as well as in democracies, the seat of sovereignty is in the people. In the United States and other free countries this is an avowed principle.

INTERNAL ASPECTS OF SOVEREIGNTY

Viewed from the standpoint of its internal organization, a sovereign state has been defined as

a body politic or a society of men united together for the purpose of promoting their mutual comfort and advantage by the joint efforts of their combined strength . . . as a self-sufficient body of persons united together in one community for the defense of their rights and for other purposes. In this sense "state" means the whole people united together in one body politic. It must be an organization of the people for political ends. It must permanently occupy a fixed territory. It must possess an organized government capable of making, and enforcing the law within the community. . . .[2]

In short, a sovereign state possesses full powers of self-government in all matters internal or domestic. It has complete control over its territories and over the people within them, other than the resident representatives of other sovereign states.

No sovereign power, apart from treaty or convention, has a legal right to exercise any control within the boundaries of another sovereign power. It is only when one sovereign state uses its powers of self-government in such a way as to cause injury within, or to interfere with the internal or domestic affairs of another, that such other may legiti-

---

[2] *Ex parte Corliss*, 114 N.W. 962, 890 (16 N.D. 470).

mately complain. Thus, the United States is justified in objecting to Canada's taking any action along the upper stretches of the Columbia River which would lessen its flow south of the Canadian border, while Canada is justified in regarding as interference in her internal affairs any attempt by the United States to oblige Canadian corporations, which are subsidiaries of United States corporations, to operate in accordance with the law of the United States.

EXTERNAL ASPECTS OF SOVEREIGNTY

Viewed from the standpoint of external relations, a sovereign state is one which other sovereign states recognize as having a stable government, capable not only of maintaining internal order, and rightfully authorized to conduct foreign affairs, but also one which will not act unduly to endanger the peace and safety of other sovereign states, and one that will extend to the persons and properties of the citizens of other sovereign states (when within its borders) the rights, privileges, and protection to which they are entitled.

EXTRATERRITORIALITY

When a sovereign state has permission to exercise governmental powers within the territories of another sovereign state, the former state is said to enjoy extraterritorial rights. The right claimed by the United States at the close of World War II to try Americans under United States law in Japan for offenses allegedly committed by them against Japanese civilians is an example.

Some extraterritorial rights are granted as matters of courtesy. Among them are the exemption of ambassadors from liability under the laws of the countries to which they are appointed, and the treating of visiting warships and the premises occupied by foreign legations as territories of the sovereign powers they represent. These and other usages of sovereign governments, although there is no central authority to enforce them, constitute international law.

Extraterritoriality played a larger part in international relations in the past than in the present. Problems of the nature which it was designed to solve still arise, but, with the decline of force as an instrument of diplomacy, it is falling into disuse. No single cause accounts for this. The Western powers are no longer dominant; the East is armed; and, with the decline of distance as an important factor, a start has been made toward the unification of laws through treaty and convention. As an example, airplanes which belong to citizens of countries which are parties to the Warsaw Convention, when engaged in international commerce, come under the terms of the convention and are not subject to the domestic laws of the signatory states.

THE RIGHT OF GOVERNMENTS TO BIND THE GOVERNED

Governments are the agencies through which organized societies exercise their collective wills. Therefore a government, to be recognized as having the right to enter into treaties, should be so established that agreements entered into by it can be justly considered as binding upon the society it purports to represent. Something more than the *claim* of authority is required; to merit continued recognition as sovereign, a government must not only be capable of acting, it must act to see that all persons subject to its rule discharge the obligations entered into on their behalf.

Great differences of opinion arise between governments of sovereign states as to whether or not the government of a newly organized state, or a new government organized within the territories of an old state, should be given recognition. Thus there are sovereign states today that refuse to recognize the Government of Israel—just as the United States for years refused to recognize the communist government of Russia and still denies recognition to the communist government of China.

DIPLOMATIC AND CONSULAR SERVICES

When two governments recognize each other as sovereign, and there is peace between them, each appoints an ambassador to represent it in the capital of the other; and each may establish consulates throughout the territories of the other.

There is no definite line of demarcation between the duties of an ambassador and those of a consul, but in general it can be said the primary function of an ambassador is to act as the agent of his government in transacting official business with the government to which he is accredited, and the function of a consul is to deal with matters of a personal nature in which the interests of private citizens are involved.

If you are a citizen of the United States traveling abroad, or if, while at home, you are transacting, or wish to transact, business with persons dwelling in countries with which the United States maintains diplomatic relations, you are privileged to make use of her consular service. The consul to whom you apply will furnish you with all available information and will use every effort to see that you get the treatment to which you are entitled under international law— under the laws of the country involved and under any treaty or treaties that such country may have entered into with the United States. If, despite the efforts of the consul, you are denied your rights, your case becomes a matter of more than personal concern. It passes into the realm of intergovernmental relations and becomes a diplomatic problem to be ironed out through diplomatic channels by the ambassador of the United States.

When you say that you are a citizen of the United States it means more than that you owe allegiance to its government and are subject to its laws; it means that when you are traveling in foreign countries, or have dealings with persons subject to their laws, you have behind you the prestige and, if need be, the power of a great sovereign state.

When one state is at war with another, when the government of one state denies recognition to that of another state, or when, for any reason, diplomatic relations between them have been broken off, each entrusts its interests in the territory of the other to the embassy of another state. The Government of Great Britain recognizes and is recognized by the governments of both Communist China and the United States. The Government of the United States does not recognize the Government of Communist China but does recognize the desirability of keeping a line of communication open to Peking. This is accomplished through arrangements between the Government of the United States and the Government of Great Britain, whereby the former makes use of the diplomatic services of the latter. For similar reasons, and in a similar way, the United States now entrusts the care of its interests in Cuba to the Swiss ambassador to Cuba.

TYPES OF GOVERNMENT

Governments fall roughly into three classes: absolute monarchies and/or dictatorships, limited or constitutional monarchies, and republics.

Under absolute monarchies and dictatorships the will of one person prevails. Such persons must, of course, command enough support to sustain them. This support may come from an organized minority rather than from the majority of the people. An absolute monarch or a dictator may draw up a set of rules relating to his own conduct, have them approved by those subservient to him, and proclaim he is giving constitutional government to his people. This is a perversion of terms. The word constitutional, as used in connection with government, signifies powers arising from the people. Thus, under a constitutional or limited monarchy the people are not subject to the arbitrary will of their monarch. They, through laws of their own making, have imposed limitations upon the power of their rulers.

Under the republican form of government the people, through the direct exercise of their sovereign powers, create their own instrumentalities of government and delineate their authority.

CONSTITUTIONAL LAW

Laws relating to the organization and functioning of governments are classified as constitutional law. Such laws may be nothing more than well-established precedents, as in the case of Great Britain, or they may be embodied in written documents, such as the Constitution of the United States and the constitutions of the several states of the American Union.

In Great Britain the powers of sovereignty are traditionally vested by the people in Parliament to be exercised as it wishes. Since Parliament is the agency which creates all other governmental agencies, there is no agency empowered to call the validity of its acts into question. It is different in the United States. Here the people have delegated some of their powers of sovereignty to the federal government, some to their state governments, and some they have reserved for themselves. This division of sovereign powers is effected through written constitutions. Hence, to understand it, some knowledge of these instruments is necessary.

Simply stated, the difference between the Constitution of the United States and the constitutions of the several states is this: The Constitution of the United States is primarily a granting or an enabling instrument, whereas the constitutions of the several states are primarily disabling or limiting instruments. This is to say, the Government of the United States can exercise only those powers which the people have expressly or impliedly delegated to it under the Constitution of the United States whereas a state government can exercise all the powers of sovereignty other than those delegated to the federal government and those denied to it by the constitution of the state.

It is well to note that there are limitations implicit in the constitutional grant of power, and that a grant of power is implicit in constitutional limitations. It may be said, therefore, that the powers of the Government of the United States are limited to those expressly or impliedly granted to it by the Constitution of the United States whereas the constitution of a state grants to the government it creates all the sovereign powers of the people other than those delegated to the federal government and those expressly reserved by the people for themselves. For example, there are no Indiana state bonds. The Constitution of the State of Indiana expressly denies to the Government of Indiana the right to create a public debt.

"A written constitution," says one court, "while in every instance a limitation upon the powers of government in the hands of its agents, is also a delegation and grant of power, and a limitation of the exercise of the power granted."[3] When this is understood, no confusion of thought arises from statements to the effect that the powers of the federal

[3] *State* v. *Braxton County Court*, 55 S.E. 382, 384; 60 W. Va. 973; 46 Tex. Cr. R. 372.

government are limited by the Constitution of the United States, or that a state constitution grants powers to the government of the state.

EXPRESSED AND IMPLIED POWERS

As references have been made, and will be made, to express and implied powers, it is necessary to say something about their nature. Express powers are easily understood; they are the powers set forth in words. Implied powers are the powers which, though not enumerated, must be used to implement, or to put into effect, the powers that are specifically granted. An implied power presupposes an express power to which it relates, and can be used only to the extent necessary to make effective use of such express power.

MAKING AND AMENDING CONSTITUTIONS

Under the republican form of government, constitutions are made and amended by the people. In the United States the constitution of a state is nothing more than a law enacted by the people of the state through the direct exercise of their sovereign power; the Constitution of the United States is a law made by the peoples of the several states acting through their state legislatures.

In the making or amending of a state constitution, the people go to the polls and vote for or against the proposal presented to them. They function as a legislative body, which as a matter of fact they are. Indeed, they constitute the highest legislative body of the land. They enact the law that creates the legislature that in turn makes all the other laws of the state. In making the Constitution of the United States the legislatures of the states acted as the agents of the peoples of the states, just as they now act in making amendments to it. An agent, it will be recalled, acts for and in the stead of the principal and is empowered to exercise discretion within the limits of the agency.

When the United States was formed, the states submitted the question of whether to join or not to join to their respective peoples. But even then a state legislature was not bound, in matters pertaining to the Constitution of the United States, by the expressed will of the majority of the citizens of the state.

The citizens of New York State voted against joining the Union, but despite this their legislature, through the exercise of its right of discretion, ratified the Federal Constitution. That this action was justified has since been affirmed by the Supreme Court of the United States through its holding that a state legislature has the power to ratify an amendment to the Federal Constitution without submitting the question as to whether or not it should do so to the voters of the state. This does not mean the Constitution of the United States is not the creation of the people of the United States, considered not as citizens of the several states but as citizens of the United States; the people are in control in that they could, if they wished, use the legal machinery now in existence to amend the Constitution so as to make the ratification of any amendment to it dependent upon the outcome of state referendums. That this has not been done signifies that the people of the United States, in their dual capacity as citizens of the several states and citizens of the United States, are content to let their state legislatures exercise their discretion as agents.

SUPREMACY OF FEDERAL LAW

After an amendment to the Constitution of the United States has been ratified by the requisite number of states, it is incorporated into the Constitution and thereby becomes part of the supreme law of the land. This is to say, the provisions of the Constitution of the United States take precedence over both federal and state laws with which they may be in conflict.

As between state and federal laws dealing with a matter over which jurisdiction has been delegated to the federal government, federal laws prevail. A state, however, may make and enforce laws dealing with matters that have been entrusted to the federal government as long as such laws are in keeping with federal laws. And, in areas in which the federal government is entitled to legislate but has not done so, a state may make and enforce any laws it wishes.

PROCUREMENT OF UNIFORM LAWS

The powers exercised by the Government of the United States are delegated powers. There are many matters with respect to which the several states retain the right to legislate. This has necessitated the enactment by the states of a multiplicity of laws relating to the same subjects. As between states, many of these statutes, together with judgments and opinions, are in conflict. Recognizing the disadvantages of this diversity, there are those who advocate the enactment of uniform laws by the states and/or the adoption of a single judicial system.

When Congress, in the opinion of the Supreme Court of the United States, acts in excess of the powers either expressly or impliedly granted to it, its acts are unconstitutional. They are void and of no effect. This prevents Congress, with the approval of the President (or over his veto), from arbitrarily and directly imposing its will upon the people of the states.

It is possible for Congress to influence state action in matters over which the states have retained control. It does this by limiting the applicability of a law passed by it, which involves "state rights," to the states which enact complementary laws. In other words, before such a law becomes applicable to a state, the state legislature must enact a law which meets the conditions or fulfills the requirements set forth in the federal law. Federal aid in the construction of highways is an outstanding example of this.

To qualify for federal aid in building roads, a state legislature must enact a law authorizing payment by the state of a percentage of the cost. The roads built must be federally approved and constructed in conformity with federal specifications. What is true of roads is (or may be) true in all areas in which federal aid is granted. This is why those who believe each state should have the right to determine its educational policies oppose federal aid to education. As Congress does not have the right to compel state legislatures to cooperate with it, it cannot, by making grants-in-aid contingent upon complementary legislation, force the states to unify their laws by the enactment of identical statutes. However, it can and does exert great influence or pressure. Federal grants-in-aid come out of the federal Treasury to which the taxpayers of all states contribute. Hence, where and when federal aid is available, the taxpayers of a noncooperating state help to finance a national program from which they receive no benefit.

Other than by taking the initiative in procuring an amendment to the Constitution of the United States, there is but one way in which the Government of the United States can proceed to force uniformity of law in the area of state jurisdiction. This is through the exercise of its treaty-making power.

THE TREATY-MAKING POWER

The President of the United States is authorized to nego-
tiate treaties, the terms of which, when ratified by the Senate, have the same legal force as the provisions of the Constitution. They become part of the supreme law of the land,
and, as such, render null and void all federal and state laws
with which they conflict. By the terms of the Warsaw Convention, to which the United States is a party, when an
airplane owned by a national of any of the signatory powers
has an accident within the United States, while engaged in
international commerce, the liability of its owner is determined under the terms of the Convention and not under
the law of the state in which the accident occurred. Thus it
is that the President, with the approval of the Senate, can,
in effect, amend the Constitution by entering into a treaty
or a convention. Those who fear the abuse of the treaty-
making power advocate amending the Constitution to transfer it to Congress. Those who oppose this action do so on
the ground that it would deprive the President—and those
who aid him in the conduct of foreign affairs—of the flexi-
bility required in carrying on international negotiations,
and would therefore prove to be detrimental to the best
interest of the United States.

CONSTITUTIONALITY

Whether or not Congress has exceeded its express or implied powers in enacting a law is a matter for the Supreme
Court of the United States to decide. Whether or not a state
legislature has exercised some power denied to it under the
constitution of the state is a question to be decided by the
supreme court of the state. When, however, a state law

raises the question as to whether or not the legislative realm of the federal government has been invaded by the state— or when the rights of the individual, not as a citizen of the state but as a citizen of the United States, are involved— the Supreme Court of the United States is the court of last resort, the court beyond which there is no appeal.

The Supreme Court of the United States, from its beginning, has declined to pass upon the constitutionality of an act of Congress prior to the question of its validity being raised as a defense in the course of a regularly litigated action. The same is true of most of the supreme courts of the states in the matter of state laws. A few, however, when asked whether or not a proposed law, if enacted, would be constitutional, have said what their decision would be. This is usually called a declaratory judgment.

Doubt as to whether or not a statute is constitutional is resolved in favor of its constitutionality. Judgments reached under a statute prior to its being declared unconstitutional stand. The matter that was in dispute is said to be *res judicata*, which means something that has been adjudicated, a matter upon which judgment has been passed, or something that is no longer open to argument.

Prior to the rendition of judgment, either litigant has the opportunity to present any objection he wishes to the proceedings, not only as to their regularity but also to the validity of the statute under which they are brought. In the absence of timely objection, that is, objection raised during the course of the proceedings, the validity of a judgment is not open to question. Thus, when the question of constitutionality is not raised, and a cause proceeds to judgment on the assumption by all the parties and the court that the statute involved is valid, the judgment cannot be attacked subsequently on constitutional grounds. This is true even though later the statute is held to be unconstitutional in another or different suit. The court assumes that a statute is constitutional until the question of its constitutionality is raised by one of the litigants.

STARE DECISIS AND THE SUPREME COURT

The power to declare the acts of Congress unconstitutional gives the Supreme Court of the United States the key position in the United States constitutional system. The laws of the United States, as distinguished from the law of the several states, are, in the last analysis, what the Supreme Court says they are. The Supreme Court has no positive legislative powers; it cannot directly enact laws. However, when a case involving the constitutionality of an act of Congress is brought before it it has the power to rule whether or not the act is to continue to be law and what interpretation is to be placed upon it by the federal courts. Taken together, these powers constitute what may be described as "negative legislative power," that is, the power to say what the law is to be by saying what cannot be law. Therefore, effective federal law is that which is embodied in the decisions of the Supreme Court. That these decisions are in effect law is due to the fact that the common law rule of *stare decisis* (which means *let the decision stand*) prevails in the federal courts. While it is to anticipate, it may not be out of place to state here that there are circumstances under which the Supreme Court can take the initiative, under a writ of *certiorari*, in bringing a matter before it for review.

Under the doctrine of *stare decisis* the lower courts of a judicial system follow the precedents established by the highest court of the judiciary. Thus a judgment of a lower court not in keeping with the prevailing precedent will, upon appeal, be overruled unless the judges composing the appeal court conclude the time has come when, in the interest of justice, the prevailing precedent should be set aside. In this event, the decision handed down by the appeal court will establish a new precedent for the future guidance of the lower courts. This is nowhere better illustrated than in the field of civil rights.[4]

THE ISSUE OF CIVIL RIGHTS

Shortly after the American Civil War, ostensibly to assure that Negroes throughout the United States would be permitted to enjoy the rights to which their liberation from slavery entitled them, the Constitution of the United States was amended to make mandatory some things which Americans theretofore had taken for granted. Among these was the proposition that all free men are entitled to the equal protection of the law. This provision, like most provisions of the Constitution, is mere statement of principle. It leaves unanswered the question, which continually arises, as to what constitutes equality under the law.

Under United States procedural law the Supreme Court interprets the Constitution. Social and economic conditions undergo continuous change. Treatment that society may at one time regard as reasonably equal may be unacceptable at another time. This necessitates, from time to time, a reinterpretation of the general provisions of the Constitution. Hence, to know what the legal rights of the individual (either white or Negro) have been in the United States at any time, it is necessary to be acquainted with the Civil Rights rulings of the Supreme Court. (This is a matter of history which we will not pursue further than is necessary

---

4 Compare the dissenting opinion in *Plessy* v. *Ferguson* with the majority opinion in *Brown* v. *Board of Education*. Both cases are set out in the appendixes.

to gain an understanding of the present legal status of the Negro. To do more would be to digress. Our present interest is in the role the law can play in expediting social reform rather than in legal detail.)

THE QUESTION OF EQUALITY

When, near the end of the last century, the question of what constitutes equal protection of the laws was presented to the Supreme Court of the United States, in *Plessy* v. *Ferguson*,[5] a case involving the use of public transportation facilities by Negroes, it ruled that a state which provided the races with separate, but physically equal, facilities had discharged its constitutional obligation. This decision made "separate but equal" the law of the land, and in the opinion of some, it would still be the law had all those affected by it placed as much emphasis upon the word equal as upon the word separate. Be this as it may, the fact is that when the question as to what constitutes equality in the matter of public service came again before the Court, in *Brown* v. *Board of Education*,[6] it took psychological as well as physical factors into consideration, and changed its position, ruling in 1954 that, in a psychological sense, separate facilities, even though physically equal, could never be equal in fact; that under the Constitution equality could mean only one and the same service.

Thus, as a matter of judge- or court-made law, the right of Negroes to attend public schools, to use public utilities, to enjoy public parks, to bask in the sun on public beaches, to swim in public swimming pools, to play on public golf

[5] *Plessy* v. *Ferguson*, 163 U.S. 537, 16 S.Ct. 1138, 41 L.Ed. 256; also see Appendix.

[6] *Brown* v. *Board of Education*, 347 U.S. 483, 74 S.Ct. 686, 98 L.Ed. 873; also see Appendix.

courses, and so forth, is the same as that of the whites. In short, segregation in these and related areas was outlawed throughout the United States by a decision of the Supreme Court.

Because the rule enunciated in *Brown* v. *Board of Education* is limited in its application to agencies of government and public callings, it left in dispute the question, already before the public, as to whether or not persons engaged in what from time immemorial had been considered to be purely private, competitive undertakings should be left free to determine their own managerial practices. Stated differently, what the Supreme Court did in the case under review was to reduce the issue of civil rights, as a matter of law, to the question of whether or not the owners of private competitive enterprises should be permitted to continue to legally discriminate between whites and Negroes in the conduct of their businesses. This is, in effect, to ask whether or not private entrepreneurs should have the legal right to choose the criterion, even though it be that of race or color, to be used by them in deciding such matters as to whom to sell or to whom not to sell.

As a problem of this kind, apart from a constitutional amendment, has to be resolved by the Supreme Court, and as no law existed at the time through the interpretation of which the Court could resolve it, those interested in having it resolved were obliged to resort to legislation. Thus it was that the so-called Civil Rights Bill of 1964 was introduced into Congress and eventually enacted into law. We use the phrase "so-called" because, in the final analysis, that to which the bill or law relates is beliefs. To claim a right is indirectly to express a belief. This being true, and because, as heretofore explained, beliefs play the leading role in what may be termed the social drama, we think the import of the 1964 Civil Rights law will be better understood if we think, for the most part, in terms of beliefs rather than in terms of rights.

The 1964 Civil Rights Bill was sponsored and vigorously supported by persons who believe that private, competitive business organizations should be compelled by law, in common with agencies of government and public utilities, to treat all men as equals in matters of business. It was opposed and vigorously campaigned against by persons who believe the Government of the United States is not entitled, under the Constitution, to interfere with the right of private citizens, as owners of property, to do as they wish with that which they own, subject only to the ancient rule that no man may use his property in any way that will interfere with other men in the reasonable enjoyment of their rights.

Despite spirited opposition, this Civil Rights Bill was passed by Congress, and, upon being signed by the President, became the law of the land. A federal law is presumed to be constitutional and binding upon all until the Supreme Court, in a case challenging its constitutionality, decrees otherwise. When the Court in such a case upholds the constitutionality of a law there is an end, at least for the time being, to all argument concerning its validity.

In the case of a federal law that vitally affects the interests of some particular group or groups, sooner or later an action will be brought in some federal district court to test its constitutionality. In the case of the Civil Rights Law of 1964, such an action could hardly have been brought sooner. Two hours after the President had signed the Civil Rights Bill at least two suits were filed challenging the constitutionality of its Public Accommodation Section. Because of the importance of the question involved, the lower federal courts acted quickly in passing these cases on to the Supreme Court, which, for the same reason, acted just as quickly, and, on the basis that interstate commerce was involved, upheld the provisions of the above controversial section.

What the Supreme Court had to decide in the two fore-going cases was simply which of the two rights claimed, or, better stated, which of the two beliefs involved (the belief that an owner should be permitted by law to do whatever he wishes to do with his property, subject only to the limitations heretofore stated, or the belief that no man should be discriminated against on the sole basis of race, color or creed) should be given legal sanction. There is nothing unique in this.

The same question, in essence, is presented to the Supreme Court in every case that is brought before it. It is only the form the question takes and the beliefs reflected in the rights claimed by the opposing parties that change. And each time the question is asked the Court must answer. This is a duty it cannot avoid. In fact, the sole purpose for which it exists is to answer, directly, questions relating to the legal priority of rights, which is, in essence, to answer the question as to which of the conflicting beliefs currently held by different groups in society shall prevail as a matter of law.

In what we will term the current civil rights cases thus far decided, the basic question has been which belief should prevail legally: the belief that the state has the right to impose segregation, or the belief that it is the right of all free men to avail themselves, on a basis of equality, of public services and/or accommodations intended for use by the public, whether publicly or privately owned.

When we look behind the question directly presented to the Supreme Court in *Brown* v. *Board of Education*, namely, whether or not segregation in the public schools of the United States was legal, we discover the real point at issue was whether or not such segregation amounted to racial discrimination. This was the indirect, basic, or underlying question the Court had to answer before it could decide whether or not separate public schools for whites and Negroes were legally allowable.

Directly stated, this question was: Does segregation as practiced in the public school system amount to racial discrimination, or does it not? When the Court convinced itself it did, it had nothing more to decide. It must then hold that separate schools, even though physically equal, could not be equal in fact. This it did. And in so doing it not only sanctioned the Christian belief in human worth, it gave new meaning to the Declaration made by the founders of the United States—among whom there were, ironically, many slave-owners—that all men are created equal.

When the Supreme Court ruled that *"The segregation of children in public schools, solely on the basis of race, even though the physical facilities and other tangible factors may be equal, deprives the children of a minority group of equal educational opportunities, and amounts to a deprivation of the equal protection of the laws guaranteed by the Fourteenth Amendment to the Federal Constitution,"* it did more than answer the question directly before it, namely, whether or not segregation in the field of public education was lawful. It indirectly answered the question as to the legality of segregation in all other publically owned and/or tax-supported institutions and activities. This is because a decision of the Supreme Court, made with respect to one governmental service, must, while it stands, be applied to all.

While the decision in *Brown* v. *Board of Education* outlawed segregation as a matter of public policy, it left those engaged in purely private enterprise legally free to refuse to deal with a person for no other reason than that of race or color. This, as we are aware, led to the enactment of the Civil Rights Law of 1964, the public accommodations section[7] of which has been held by the Supreme Court to be constitutional.[8]

The enactment of the 1964 Civil Rights Law by Congress, and the upholding of the constitutionality of the Public Accommodation Section by the Supreme Court, gave to the Negro the statutory right to demand services from businesses engaged in interstate commerce. Whether or not this right, in the strict meaning of the word, can be called a civil right is open to doubt. To the extent that both Congress and the Supreme Court relied upon the Commerce Clause of the Constitution, the issue of civil rights (the core of which is human rights) has been evaded. Not even a partial answer has been given to the question as to whether or not the Constitution of the United States entitles a Negro, as a matter of human equality, to receive the same treatment as a white man in all matters other than social relations. And this is the question which Congress should have dealt with and with which the Supreme Court could have dealt with had it seen fit. (This is in keeping with the concurring opinion of Justice Douglas in the case of *Heart of Atlanta Motel, Inc.* v. *U.S.*,[9] which opinion, in our thinking, like the dissenting opinion of Justice Harlan in *Plessy* v. *Ferguson*, is more important that that of the majority in that it is prophetic.)

All that Congress has thus far provided and all that the Supreme Court has thus far decreed is that those engaged in interstate commerce shall not practice racial discrimination.

To deprive those engaged in interstate commerce of the right to practice racial discrimination is to entitle Negroes

---

[7] Civil Rights Law of 1964, Public Accommodation Section (Title 2). See Appendix.

[8] *Heart of Atlanta Motel Inc.* v. *U.S.* 85 S.Ct. 348.

[9] 85 S.Ct. 348.

to the same treatment as white men in this area. However, this does not amount to racial equality. A right that accrues to one group as a result of a restriction placed on another group is not the same as a right directly recognized.

Regardless of its true intent, Congress in framing the Public Accommodation Section of the 1964 Civil Rights Law in a way to assure its constitutionality under the Commerce Clause, made it, at least in form, a law to promote interstate commerce. What is needed is a law to directly supplement the Moral Law in making socially effective the belief that racial discrimination should not be practiced. The significance of this becomes clearly apparent when it is realized that a Negro who wished to bring a lawsuit under the Public Accommodation Section would be obliged to predicate his case upon the fact that he was engaged in interstate commerce and not upon the fact that one of his rights as a human being had been violated. And this, together with the fact that private persons engaged wholly in *intrastate* activities are legally free to discriminate between the races, will remain true as long as Congress and the Supreme Court find it possible and expedient to bypass the "equal protection before the law" provision of the Fourteenth Amednment and to take refuge behind the Commerce Clause when ostensibly dealing with human rights.

Important as the foregoing matters are, they are but preliminary. To summarize: The desegragationists have won a legislative skirmish; they have won the opening legal battle; and they are favored to win any that follow; but victory in the moral campaign, upon which the establishment of peace ultimately depends, is yet a long way off. How far depends less upon future legislation and the ardency with which present legislation is enforced than upon the conduct of those it is designed to benefit. The future of the Negro now lies largely in his own hands.

Human nature being what it is, it is not surprising that the judgment outlawing segregation in public schools and the judgments based upon it, establishing the legal right of Negroes to mingle freely with whites in all public places, and the provisions of the Civil Rights Law that forbid practices which would result in racial discrimination, have caused some discontent. Nor is it surprising that this is especially true in areas in which segregation has long been practiced.

Those who believe in segregation as a continuing policy bitterly resent having desegregation imposed upon them either by court decree or through legislation. But these people are not alone. Many persons, in the South and elsewhere, who believe desegregation to be, in the end, both desirable and inevitable, are numbered among the opponents of present policy. Neither of these groups is to be indicted upon moral grounds. The person who, because of his convictions, opposes desegregation is relatively just as moral as the person who, because of his convictions, supports it.

LAW HAS NO MAGIC

Law possesses no magic to change beliefs. Beliefs, under the operation of the moral law, control conduct. The problem of race relations therefore is not to be solved at the legal level. Apart from the moral law, there is no ultimate solution. Civil rights will cease to be a difficult problem in the United States only when the belief that individual worth does not depend upon the color of one's skin is widely and strongly enough held that the moral law, acting upon it, will compel conduct on the part of the majority of Americans in keeping with the declaration that all men are created equal. As the ultimate solution of the race problem is a matter of belief and not of law, the question arises as to what part, if any, sovereign power can play in the creation of beliefs.

LAW AND SOCIAL REFORM

In our discussion of the origin of beliefs in what is right and what is wrong, and in the analysis of the concepts of absolute and relative morality, it was said that beliefs arise either from revelation of the purposes of nature or from human experience. It was assumed there are purposes in nature and it was agreed that man has no alternative to accepting these purposes as good in the ultimate and absolute sense. Man was recognized as the highest creation of nature. Hence, it was decided, the purpose of nature must be to promote his welfare. On these bases it was concluded that, when the beliefs of men are in keeping with the purposes of nature, and his acts are in keeping with his beliefs, his acts are absolutely moral.

No one but a cynic would hold the welfare of men to be promoted through international and interracial strife, hence the all-but-universal belief in the desirability of peace. At least since the time of the Prophet Isaiah, the attainment of peace has been accepted, on the basis of revelation, as being a moral objective, and the validity of this belief has been confirmed by experience. If men, as finite beings, are justified in holding any acts to be absolutely moral, acts which will ultimately advance the cause of peace must be numbered among them.

The law can do nothing to speed revelation and thereby intensify and spread the belief that the rights to which a man is entitled do not depend upon the color of his skin. The problem of revelation, like that of absolute morality, lies beyond the scope of law; both come within the field of religion. However, insofar as beliefs in what is right and what is wrong are the outcome of experience, the law can play a part. It can create an environment which gives rise to experiences which those subject to the environment otherwise would not have.

The fact that an experience is forcibly imposed does not alter the relationship between experience and belief. Many beliefs arise out of experience. The environment created by a law influences the thinking of all persons subjected to it. If a statute enacted by a democratic legislature creates socially undesirable conditions, it will fall into disrepute and eventually be repealed. On the other hand, if the conditions created by a statute are recognized as conducive of the social good, it will lead to the intensification and wider acceptance of the belief which led to its enactment.

When allowance is made for emotional factors, the experience of the South, following the abolition of slavery, illustrates the function of law in social reform. It is now quite generally recognized that the question of slavery did not enter directly into the Civil War until President Lincoln issued his proclamation freeing the slaves. After this, but not before, the Civil War may be regarded as an action to enforce a law designed to impose upon people accustomed to slavery the experience of living in a slaveless society. No one suggests that the people now living in what were once slave states would reestablish slavery if they were free to do so. Private property in human beings is taboo on moral grounds *or* as a matter of consent. In this respect, Negroes and whites are recognized as equals. Statistical proof is lacking, but reason affirms that experiences traceable to the proclamation freeing the slaves hastened general acceptance throughout the United States of the belief that no man should be regarded as a chattel.

It is not our purpose to argue the pros and cons of any issue, but, if it is true that the environment created by the outlawing of slavery hastened the coming in the South of the widespread belief in the right of all men to be free, is there not reason to hope that the application of the rule in *Brown* v. *Board of Education* and the upholding and enforcement of the provisions of the Civil Rights Law will create an environment in which belief in the equality of men, as equality is conceived of in the Declaration of Independence and the Constitution of the United States, will come soon to be accepted generally throughout the nation? This equality is not that of either mind or body. These are matters of individual endowment. There are degrees of physical strength and mental powers, but there are no degrees of humanity. Being human is the factor that lifts all men above the level of the brute. Men are equal only in that they are human, but this is sufficient in itself to entitle all to equal protection and equal opportunity as a matter of law.

The chief argument of those who oppose desegregation is that the Negro is not ready for equality of treatment. They point to the progress he has made toward this goal since his emancipation, and many sincerely believe forced desegregation will retard, rather than hasten, its realization. Because there is in this an implied acceptance of the principle of desegregation by these segregationists, we quote the following with approval.

The law must be an educational force as well as a force, and a moral force, too. Official enforcement efforts do not meet the full obligation of the executive to the law unless they include something more than the use of the policeman's stick. They must assert with equal power what in this case I believe to be true—that our developing constitutional law of equality for all is right; that it expresses the strongest force in American life, our commitment to the corpus of ideals represented by the Declaration of Independence and the Constitution; and at some level of consciousness or unconsciousness, silently or openly, all our people, including our brother of the South, know this, believe it, and will in the end accept it.[10]

---

10 Eugene V. Restow, "The Supreme Court and the People's Will," *Notre Dame Lawyer*, Vol. XXXIII, No. 4 (August, 1958), p. 596.

Chapter 5

LAW AND

ECONOMIC SYSTEMS

ECONOMIC GOALS AND TECHNIQUES

The purpose of all economic systems is to satisfy the material needs of the peoples they serve. They do this by converting the natural and human resources at their disposal into goods and services. These they divide among their peoples. The economist calls these processes production and distribution.

Production consists of changing natural resources into forms in which they, or the services derived from them, may be consumed by man. The types of goods and services produced vary according to the needs of the people for whom they are intended, but the purposes for which they are produced are the same. Between economic systems, the techniques differ greatly: some are highly advanced; some are deplorably primitive; some economic systems are young and flexible and welcome change; some are old and inflexible and resist, on moral grounds, any departure from age-old practices.

Economic systems at or about the same level of development employ essentially the same techniques. Russia and the United States evidence this. Russia, on the whole, is less advanced technically than the United States, but there is no reason to think her better equipped industrial plants would suffer greatly from comparison with those of the United States.

The economic goals of communistic and/or socialistic

75

societies, as represented by Russia, are the same as those of free enterprise or capitalistic societies, as represented by the United States. They use the same industrial techniques. In what then do they differ? The answer is they differ in the legal institutions through which they operate.

As we understand them, communistic economic systems are based wholly, at least in theory—and socialistic economic systems are based largely—upon public property, whereas free enterprise or capitalistic economic systems are theoretically based, wholly and practically, largely upon private property. To get the meaning and understand the significance of this it is necessary to know something about the nature of property.

NATURE OF PROPERTY

In the legal sense, property consists of rights, not of things. To say something is the property of someone means that society has given that person the right to exercise control over it. This is the positive aspect of property. The negative is that when society recognizes the right of one person to exercise control over a thing it thereby recognizes the duty of all other persons not to interfere unreasonably with the exercise of that right.

The positive nature of rights and the negative nature of duties are reflected in the statement that the law grants rights and imposes duties. Taken literally, this statement is misleading, if not inaccurate. With the exception of rights reflecting duties created by law, such as the right to expect persons using the highways of the United States to drive to the right, rights are of moral origin. They are recognized as law only when those who make the law come to believe the physical enforcement of them to be in the public interest.

Legal duties are the opposites of legal rights. Just as in accounting there is a debit for every credit, there is in law a duty for every right. Men tend to be more conscious of rights than of duties. Therefore property is commonly defined as the right to exercise control over things.

Because the right to exercise control is manifested in many ways, property is sometimes said to consist not of one but of many rights; that is, it is conceived of as a bundle of rights. Thus when a zoning ordinance forbids the use of land for some specified purpose, it is thought of as depriving the owner of one of many property rights rather than as a limitation upon the exercise of a single right.

KINDS OF PROPERTY

The thing to which the right to control attaches, or the thing to which the rights of property attach, may be either tangible, as in the case of an automobile, or intangible, as in the case of a copyright, patent, or right to receive something, such as the amount of a debt.

When the state has the right to exercise absolute control over a thing, that thing is public property. When the state recognizes the right of the individual to exercise control over a thing, subject only to the superior right of the state, the thing is private property. Inasmuch as private property rights in an organized society or state are those which the state recognizes, all property, in its inception, may be thought of as having been public property.

The nature or quality of a thing is in no way affected by the classification under which it falls. The nationalization of the coal mines of Great Britain or the taking over of the Suez Canal by Egypt had no affect on these things as such. The mines and the canal underwent no change. All that happened was that controls which were formerly exercised by individuals are now exercised by governments. What was private property is now public.

In ordinary conversation it is convenient and usual to speak of material things as property, but, when legal matters are involved, it must be remembered the essence of property is the right to control and not the thing controlled.

THE SUBJECT MATTER OF CONTRACTS

Property rights are the subject matter of contracts. Contracts consist of sets of promises that meet certain requirements. A person who makes such a promise places himself under legal duty to fulfill it and gives to the person to whom it is made the right to demand its fulfillment. Every exchange of promises creates moral rights and duties, but only an exchange that can be reduced to a good offer and valid acceptance is legally binding; that is, amounts to a contract.

In the early days of the law, judges thought property consisted wholly of tangible things. Unless that which was involved in a dispute was something objective, something that could be seen and felt, something tangible, the courts held there was nothing with which the law could deal.

The right to receive something in the future is intangible yet it may be of greater value than the present right to exercise control over some tangible thing. A bond certificate evidencing the promise of the United States to pay $10,000 ten years hence is of more value to the holder than an ordinary ten-year-old automobile.

From time immemorial, the making of a promise has been recognized as giving the promisee a moral right and imposing upon the promisor a moral duty, but it was not until judges began to think in terms of rights, rather than in terms of things, that simple promises were brought within the purview of the law. Not until then could the law of contract, which is indispensable to the American way of life, develop.

PROPOSITIONS TO BE EVALUATED

Before comparing the American economic system with that of Russia, it is desirable to evaluate two propositions. The first is that in the United States the state exists for the people and not the people for the state, whereas in Russia the people exist for the state and not the state for the people. The second is that apart from private property there can be no political freedom, or that public property is a concomitant of tyranny.

INDIVIDUAL v. STATE RIGHTS

As believers in free enterprise, we agree government exists in the United States for the benefit of the people and not the people for the benefit of government. This does not mean that in the United States the rights of individuals take precedence over the rights of the government or the state. Rights are of two kinds, personal rights and property rights, and the latter are of primary interest when comparing economic systems.

Private property, or the right to exercise control over things, is enjoyed by all citizens of the United States and by citizens of all countries not at war with the United States. But the right is not absolute: it does not extend to everything; and those things to which it does extend are held by the owners subject to the superior legal rights of the state. The right of the state to take private property for public use is superior to the right of the owner to retain it. The right of the state to regulate, that is, to place restrictions upon the use and manner of use of private property when the welfare of the public requires it, takes precedence over the rights of the owner. And the right of the state to tax, by which it has the power to take and sell private property if taxes are not paid, results in the owner losing all his rights. The effect of the tax sale is to transfer the property rights to the buyer.

"AMERICAN WAY" IS NOT THE ONLY DEMOCRATIC WAY

The strength of a nation depends primarily upon the strength of the belief of its citizens in its governmental institutions. The American people believe firmly in their form of government and in their economic system, which they, on the whole, think of as being one and inseparable. Indeed, this conviction is so pronounced that many feel all the problems of the world, economic and otherwise, are to be solved by establishment of their form of government throughout the world.

From the domestic point of view, the belief of Americans that their way is the only democratic way, and that apart from private property there can be no political freedom, has—inasmuch as "The American Way" has nothing to fear from comparison with other ways—much to commend it. But it is a blind, fallacious belief which, when either expressed or implied, is resented by peoples who believe themselves to be just as free as any others.

The United States is not the only country in which the people by free elections choose representatives to sit as members of their legislatures and make their laws. In the United States the people determine by their votes who shall sit in Congress, but neither they nor those whom they elect to the House of Representatives have any voice in the selection and appointment of the various secretaries who, with the President, constitute the Cabinet—or the Executive, the Administration, or the Government.

In the United States, the President and his "understudy," the Vice President, whose official standing has never been clearly defined, are the only members of the administration or government for whom the people vote. All other members are appointed by the President with the approval of the Senate. They are not chosen from among the elected representatives of the people; they are neither Congressmen nor Senators; their tenure of office does not depend upon the will of Congress; apart from impeachment proceedings neither they nor the President can be deprived of office. In short, the executive branch of government in the United States is not responsible for its acts to the elected representatives of the people. Because of this the United States is said to have representative but not responsible government.

A responsible government, which of necessity is representative, is one formed by the leader who commands the support of the majority of the members of an elected legislature, house, or assembly. He must choose the members of his cabinet, executive, administration, or government from among the members of the house or assembly, and each member, as chosen, must resign his seat and go back to his constituency or district and be reelected before he can serve both as the representative of such constituency or district in the legislature and as a member of the government.

The head of a responsible government is the leader of the party having the support of the majority of the members of the legislature. Hence a responsible government can remain in office only as long as it commands the support of a majority of the elected representatives of the people. When it loses the confidence of the legislature, it must resign.

Where responsible government exists, as in Canada, the executive branch cannot continue to be of one political persuasion and the legislative branch of another, as in the United States. A responsible government is, therefore, more directly amenable to the will of the people than is a representative government, and, inasmuch as amenability is a test of democracy, a responsible government must be considered more democratic.

The above is not written in disparagement; it is intended merely as background for the statement that in Great Britain, where they have responsible government, the policy of public ownership of the means of production and the socialization of public services has been put widely into effect without interfering in any way with democratic political processes. The nationalization of British coal mines and the socialization of British medicine by a labor government did not prevent the British people from voting that government out of office when they came to believe that, at least for the time being, socialization had been carried far enough. This is not an argument for public ownership; it is to direct attention to the fact that socialistic economic policies may be compatible with political freedom, and that, if they are rejected, ultimately, in Great Britain or elsewhere, it will be on economic rather than on political grounds.

PUBLIC PROPERTY IS NOT A CONCOMITANT OF TYRANNY

There is no generic connection between private property and political democracy, or between public property and tyranny. Public property is not incompatible with political democratic processes, and private property is not unknown to tyrannies. It would appear that private property played a relatively greater part in the lives of the Colonials, who rebelled against the tyranny of George III, than it plays in the lives of the people of the United States today.

PRIVATE v. PUBLIC PROPERTY

Both democracies and tyrannies are confronted with the question as to what should be publicly owned and what should be left, or placed, in private hands. To understand this question, but not to answer it (since the answer to be given is dependent upon time and place), it is necessary to distinguish between goods that are essential to the life of the individual in possession and goods used by the possessor in the production of other goods upon which his life does not depend. This classification is to be distinguished from the economic classification of things under the heading of producers' goods (or economic capital) and consumer goods. It differs from this classification in that one bow and arrow, which is producers' goods or economic capital, may be essential to the owner as a means of livelihood, while a factory for the production of bows and arrows, clearly economic capital, would not be. This is not to say either that individuals should not produce goods for exchange or that all implements of production should be publicly owned. The question is not one of either private or public ownership; it is rather one of the question of how much of the one and how much of the other is for the public good.

The distinction between goods essential to the survival of the individual and goods used in the production of things which the producer does not personally need takes into consideration both the intuitive or natural, and the rational or conventional, basis of private property. This, since private property is described in the American Declaration of Independence as an inalienable right, may well cause Americans to ask: Just what does the term inalienable right mean?

Inalienable rights are based on intuition. Belief in them arises out of the nature of man. They are universally asserted. They, therefore, are rights which no society can indefinitely deny its members. Rational or conventional rights are those believed in because of experience. They are asserted only where they are believed in and only as long as the controlling elements in the society involved believes the assertion of them to be in its best interests. The right to private property is here in point.

With respect to things essential to survival, the right of private property is instinctively asserted throughout the kingdom of living things. The birds defend their nests and feeding areas; the animals defend their dens and food supplies.

Man, as an animal, acts intuitively, and doubtless throughout history has asserted property rights in the case of things essential to his survival. Man, as an intellectual, acts on the basis of reason. Thus, when he developed the capacity to visualize his future needs, and when individuals discovered they could provide for the satisfaction of their wants by exercising control over the factors of production, those strong enough to do so brought these factors under their control.

Private property rights, insofar as they are essential to the survival of the person who holds them, and his dependents, can be justified on the ground of natural or inalienable rights; private property rights in producers' goods and consumers' goods in excess of personal and family needs must find their justification in objective benefits in which mankind in general shares. To summarize, clarify, and emphasize what this involves, we make reference to the American and Russian revolutions.

THE AMERICAN REVOLUTION

The American Revolution brought about the formation of a government whose legislative branch is composed wholly of elected representatives and whose executive branch is headed by the elected representative of the people. The representatives of the people, the President, the Vice President, the members of the Senate (except those appointed to complete the terms of Senators who die in office), and the members of the House of Representatives are chosen in free elections to serve for limited periods of time. The Presidency, the Senate, and the House of Representatives are continuing institutions, the personnel or personnels of which are subject to periodic change at the will of the voters. In this sense the American people are masters of their government. (It is to be recognized, however, that this mastery does not extend to the day-to-day activities of government.) Their control is not immediate, but ultimate.

The Constitution of the United States has been described by jurists as "the supreme and paramount law,"[1] as "the fundamental law of the land,"[2] and as the law by which "the judges in every state are bound . . . anything in the constitution or laws of their own state notwithstanding."[3] It is in fact not only law, it is the law by which the validity of all other laws in the United States is in the end determined. This, however, is not inconsistent with the view, held by some, that the Constitution is more than law since, as is said in *State* v. *Harden*,[4] it, "for the most part, may be con-

---

[1] *Rice* v. *Palmer*, 96 S.W. 396, 398.

[2] *Henry* v. *State*, 39 So. 856, 893.

[3] *Atkinson* v. *Woodmansee*, 74 Pac. 640, 641.

[4] *State* v. *Harden*, 58 S.E. 715–18.

strued as a great compact or agreement, entered into by all the people of the state, for and on behalf of themselves and those who shall come after them, until such time as it is abolished, changed or modified."[5]

Whether it be law or compact matters little; it came into being through action by the people; it exists at their will; and it can be amended by them at any time. It is under it that they elect their President, their Vice President, their Senators, and their Representatives in the House of Representatives to act as their agents in the conduct of their government for specified periods of time. Apart from impeachment proceedings, the people can in no way control the conduct of these agents during the terms for which they were elected. They can, however, terminate their agencies by denying them reelection. Government, then, in the United States is not subservient to the people in the ordinary meaning of the word. It is subservient only in the sense it takes the form the people want it to take and is carried on, for the most part, by persons of their choosing.

The founders of the Government of the United States recognized that government is inherently autocratic. They understood that even a government deriving its powers directly from the governed has the right to exercise all the rights of sovereignty not denied to it by the source from which it derives its powers. The Bill of Rights was incorporated into the Constitution of the United States to deprive government of the right—which it otherwise could possess—to exercise certain enumerated powers.

THE RUSSIAN REVOLUTION

In contrast with the American Revolution, the Russian Revolution brought about the formation of a government

---

[5] *Atkinson* v. *Woodmansee, supra.*

which has fallen into the hands of a powerful minority group known as the Communist Party. The leaders of this group, in the tradition of leaders who have established governments by force rather than through consent, permit no criticism and tolerate no opposition. They reject the Judean–Christian ethic which, through the recognition of individual worth, gives rise to democratic governments, and they maintain by practice—whether or not they propound the doctrine—that the individual exists to be used by government for the aggrandizement of the state. In Russia, as in other countries where this belief prevails, the rights of the individual are limited to those which do not interfere with the concentration of power in the hands of the government. Property, or the right to control things, is power, whether in the hands of individuals or in the hands of government. Hence a government in the hands of those who believe it is the first function of government to increase the power and prestige of the State will carry the policy of public ownership further than will a government in the hands of those who believe in public ownership only insofar as it is necessary to maximize individual welfare.

BELIEFS AND POLICIES

In comparing the legal foundations of communism, as represented by Russia, with free enterprise, as represented by the United States, it is necessary to remember it is beliefs that give rise to policies, not policies that give rise to beliefs. There is, of course, a reciprocal relationship of great significance. Beliefs are influenced by the results which flow from the implementation of policies.

The belief of the Russians in public property did not arise from their having had experience with it; they have come to have it because of their belief in it. In like manner, the belief in private property inherited by Americans did not develop as the result of their ancestors enjoying the benefits of it. The right of the common man to exercise control over things is asserted and established as a matter of law only after the controlling element in a society comes to believe in it, or, if you wish, only after those who believe in it come to be the controlling element in their society. How long and to what extent public property will continue to be the rule in Russia, and how far and to what extent private property will continue to be the rule in the United States depend upon how satisfactory the results achieved by these systems are to the peoples who live under them. This is a matter for sovereign determination. In the last analysis, the people are the seat of sovereignty. Hence it is appropriate for us to inquire briefly into how the Russian theory of public property and the American theory of private property are working out in practice.

THE TENDENCY TO CONVERGE

Reports coming out of Russia indicate the policy of the leaders of the Russian Revolution, based on the belief that all but the most personal things should be public property, has encountered such opposition that the scope of private property is being gradually widened there. On the other hand, in the United States, not only are more and more private property rights being denied through governmental control but more and more people are coming to believe in the desirability of public ownership. This appears to be true not only in fields where adequate service cannot be supplied at a profit but in some other fields as well. The result is that private property is playing an ever-decreasing role in the economy of this country. Thus the United States and Russia, starting from opposite extremes, the one believing that private and the other that public property best serves the interests of society, are advancing from opposite directions toward a common meeting ground.

Because of the discovery of new uses of natural resources and because of changes in techniques, stable equilibrium between private and public property may never be established. To postulate it is to postulate a static society, and this, due to discovery and invention, cannot be reasonably foreseen. Nonetheless, a relatively stable adjustment between the two may well be possible.

THE COLD WAR

The extent to which private property rights will come to be recognized in countries which now have communistic economies, the degree to which public ownership will be expanded in countries which describe their economic systems as free enterprise, and the decisions of backward, awakening countries as to which of the systems they will adopt all depend largely upon the comparative accomplishments of the two systems represented by Russia and by the United States. These two countries are aware of this. National prestige is at stake. Thus each, by emphasizing its material accomplishments, seeks to intensify the nationalism of its people and to win other peoples to its way of life.

In the battle of ideologies, or the "Cold War," little distinction is made between that which is political and that which is economic. Russian propaganda creates the impression that those who wish to avoid being exploited by private owners must adopt the Russian political system, implying that public ownership of the means of production is not possible under the American form of government. American propaganda leaves the impression that "government of the people, for the people, by the people" is possible only for those who base their economic systems on private property. No one explains that the right to determine what shall be privately owned and what shall be publicly owned is of the essence of political freedom, and that in a democracy it is the people who make the laws which determine the nature of their economic system.

For self-evident reasons, public ownership has a strong and direct appeal for the poverty-stricken masses of the world. So great is it, in fact, that these masses, if left in ignorance of the real nature of democratic government, may join the Communist Bloc in the mistaken belief that this is necessary in order to avoid having an economic system wholly motivated and controlled by the quest for profit.

The failure of the West to make clear that economic systems are merely matters of law and that peoples who make their own laws can have any type of economic system they wish gives the East a needless advantage. Reason dictates the threat of communist world domination would be diminished if those over whom communist nations seek domination were well enough informed to know they do not have to adopt the form of government now characteristic of communist countries in order to enjoy the benefits (if any) of communist economic experiments.

ECONOMIC PROCESS

The economic process can be visualized as a kind of circular flow. As producers, the members of an economic system are continually pouring raw materials and labor into the flow and continually withdrawing from it the finished goods and services they need. In Russia and other communist countries, decisions as to what individuals, as producers, shall contribute to the flow, and decisions as to what they in total, if not as individuals, may withdraw as consumers, are made by the State. In the United States and other free-enterprise countries such decisions are made by the people through the legal institution of contract.

HOW COMMUNISTIC ECONOMIC SYSTEMS FUNCTION

Economic systems based on public ownership—as well as those based on private property—are characterized by the division of labor, or specialized production. Each economic system therefore, regardless of its nature, is faced with two basic problems. These are (1) the determination of the type of productive activities in which its members, as individuals, may specialize, and (2) the providing of a system of exchange whereby the goods and services produced are distributed among the people as a whole. These are managerial problems and, as management is a function of ownership, the manner of their solutions depends upon the nature of the ownership involved.

In Russia, where public ownership is the rule, the solution of the first problem is attempted through central planning. There they have a central agency of government which determines what, where, when, and how much of each commodity and service is to be produced. In deciding this the planning agency automatically determines the distribution of labor both industrially and geographically throughout Russia. This is axiomatically true since the plan drawn up by the central agency depends for its implementation upon the labors of the people. As a corollary of this, the government, to assure such implementation, must have the power to assign each individual to the performance of some specific task.

The very existence of this governmental power is repugnant to Americans. It is to be remembered, however, that it is one thing to possess a power and quite another to exercise it. Regardless of the degree of regimentation which may have characterized the Russian economic life in the early aftermath of the Russian Revolution, there is now some reason to believe that the Russian people in general, though subject to what we term economic conscription, are not regimented to the extent that many people blindly believe them to be. As we understand it, the Russians are generally privileged (it is not their right) to choose the state-owned industry in which they wish to work just as long as the choices are made so as to bring about the distribution of labor necessary to put the central economic plan into effect. To resort once more to analogy, the privilege afforded the Russians to make economic choices bears resemblance to the privilege afforded Americans to choose the branch of service in which they wish to serve as long as the required balance is maintained.

If our analogy is true, economic matters in Russia are subject to at least as much regimentation as military matters are in the United States and this, by American standards, is an unjustifiable encroachment upon economic freedom. (Unless the Russian people are, to apply the words of Franklin, so corrupt as to need despotic government.)[6]

As in the case of the first problem, the Russian solution to the second is, in the final analysis, a matter of State decree. The State retains title to all capital or producers' goods and all implements of war. Consumers' goods are purchased from the State with wages paid by the State at rates fixed by the State. It is to be noted that exchanges of goods and services in Russia as in the United States are effected through the use of a medium of exchange and that the individual in Russia is privileged to spend his income in any

[6] See p. 36, Morals and Government.

way he wishes. His opportunity to choose, however, is limited almost wholly to the goods and services produced and sold by the Russian Government. Thus, the distribution of purchases in Russia as in the United States under capitalism reflects the relative importance attached by the consumers to different goods. This is an important factor taken into consideration by the Russian central planning agency. In theory, therefore, consumer influence on production is the same in Russia as in the United States. In practice, however, there are important differences.

In the United States those who direct industrial processes make their own decisions. They are in direct contact with consumers and become immediately aware of changes in consumer demand. There is little or no lag. Hence, the difficulty of keeping production in line with consumption is reduced to a minimum. In Russia those who direct industrial production do not make decisions with respect to the nature and amounts of things to be produced. The consumers' influence is transmitted through government channels encumbered with red tape, to the central planning agency to be taken into consideration by it when it next changes its production schedules. Thus, there is a lag (probably prolonged by the fact that those who do the planning do not stand to benefit directly from haste) that may and has resulted in supply and demand getting badly out of adjustment. Then, too, in the United States when an individual recognizes that there is a need for some new and different product, he is free to embark immediately upon the production and sale of it. And, since he stands to profit personally from his enterprise, the likelihood is that he will do so. In Russia such a commodity could not be made available to the public until the production of it had been provided for in the general or overall economic plan. And since, barring departure from professed communist practice, no one is entitled to personal gain or profit, those engaged in the promotion or development of new products are without material incentive to accelerate their efforts. And what is true in the field of new products is also true in the field of improvements in the productive process.

The above and other differences that explain why the economic system of the United States is, on the whole, more efficient than that of Russia, arise out of the differences in their laws and not out of the differences either in the nature of the tasks performed or in the techniques employed in their performance. This and not the differences as such between the economic system of Russia and the United States is what we wish to emphasize. The fact that these and all other economic systems rest upon legal foundations is one of the important, if not the most important fact (apart from the fact that laws reflect beliefs), to be taken into consideration when studying the subject of law and society. In the last analysis, of course, the differences between the laws of Russia and the laws of the United States are attributable to the differences in beliefs.

In Chapter 2 we defined liberty as the right of the individual to act in accordance with his own beliefs, that is, freedom to do as he pleases. We might well have defined it as the right of an individual to make choices and act upon them. This has economic connotation. Hence, we may say that since the individual in the United States has the all but unlimited right as opposed to privilege, to make and act upon economic choice, the economy of the United States is properly described as free. Whereas, in Russia where the field within which the individual may exercise the privilege as opposed to the right, to make and act upon economic choices is subject always to the right of the government to override them, there may be a semblance of economic freedom, but there is in truth a controlled economy. The criterion used here may be used in classifying any and all economic systems.

HOW FREE-ENTERPRISE ECONOMIC SYSTEMS FUNCTION

Where the belief is widely held, as in the United States, that those who are free to serve their own economic interests best serve the economic interests of society, the problems incident to the production and distribution of economic goods are solved in ways entirely different from the ways in which they are solved by the Russian people. Here —where the right of individuals to make economic choices and to act upon them is curtailed by law only when their belief in the rights of their fellow men is not strong enough to prompt them under the operation of the moral law to act in the social interest—the control and direction of economic activities is achieved through the operation of the legal institution of contract, which is ancillary to the institution of private property.

The importance of the individual in the contemplation of American law is nowhere more apparent than in its recognition of private property. It is this that places control over natural resources and capital goods largely in private hands, and that leaves the owners free, insofar as they do not betray their trust, to use them as they wish. The word trust is used advisedly. The right of private property in things in excess of individual needs is not recognized by law for the benefit of the owner only. The justification for it is that through its operation a society derives the greatest possible benefit from the utilization of its material and human resources. Hence it is safe to assume that this recognition will continue in the United States, and elsewhere, only as long as and to the extent that those into whose hands it places economic responsibility produce results which the public accept as being superior to those which it believes would be achieved under public ownership.

THE RIGHT TO TRANSFER RIGHTS

Inherent in the institution of private property is the right to transfer rights. This right can be exercised by the owner through the making of gifts or by entering into contracts. In contrasting communistic and capitalistic societies, gifts may be ignored. This is because capitalistic countries rely mainly upon contracts to control and direct their economic activities. Americans who do not understand this may be firm believers in the American economic way, but, as blind believers they cannot explain its advantages to others, and as a result, when exposed to communist propaganda, may be led into doubt.

FREEDOM OF CONTRACT AND THE INDIVIDUAL

It is hard to overemphasize the part played by contract in the lives of individual Americans. When an individual works for only one employer the contract between him and his employer determines the amount of his income. When an individual is in business for himself, his income, apart from what he produces for his own consumption, is the outcome of a series of contracts. It is through purchases that he gets his place of business, his raw materials or merchandise, and his labor force. And it is through sales that he disposes of his product, be it goods or services. If his sales contracts bring in more money than is required to pay the debts created by his purchase contracts, he has a profit. This is his income. It is to be noted that the application of what is said here is not confined to businessmen; the same is true of all persons independently engaged in economic pursuits.

The part played by contract is not limited to the procurement of an individual's income. It is through contract that individuals dispose of their income. It makes no difference what the recipient of a monetary income desires, he procures it through contract. He contracts with the grocer for food, with a dealer for a car, with the theater for entertainment, and so on throughout the long list of his needs. If his income is more than is required for the present, he saves the excess (unless he is a hoarder) by entering into contracts. He may contract with a savings bank or other savings institutions. He may purchase legal reserve life insurance, an annuity, or something he thinks will serve as a "storehouse" of value, such as diamonds. Contracts are encountered everywhere. It therefore behooves every American, from the practical as well as from the cultural standpoint, to know how contracts are made, how they are interpreted, and how they are enforced.

FREEDOM OF CONTRACT AND SOCIETY

From the standpoint of the individual living in the United States or other free-enterprise countries, the importance of the law of contract is great, but from the standpoint of society it may well be considered even greater. Under free enterprise the people, after deciding what goods and services they wish to consume, proceed, through contract, to bring about the production of them. In the custom trade this is evident. In production in anticipation of demand it is less evident but nonetheless true.

Let us take the automobile industry as an example of the above. When a buyer contracts for a car of his choice, he in effect "votes" for the production of another one of the same style and make. The dealer from whom he made his purchase, needing to replenish his stock, contracts with the manufacturer for a replacement. The manufacturer in his turn contracts for materials, parts, and the necessary labor to produce it. Those who supply the materials and parts needed by the manufacturer contract, in their turn, for the needed raw materials and labor.

What is true in the automobile industry is true elsewhere. Thus it is that the wishes of the people in free-enterprise countries are reflected back, through a series of contracts, to determine the purposes for which the resources of these countries are used. There is no central planning and no issuance of governmental decrees.

We chose the automobile industry for purpose of illustration because the influence of consumer decisions on production has been very evident in the United States in recent years. The increase in the number of small foreign automobiles sold in the United States in the late 1950s, combined with the sales records set by the American-made Studebaker *Lark* and Rambler *American*, caused the "Big Three" automobile manufacturers in the United States to put a plethora of small or compact cars into competition. In the beginning, these cut heavily into the sales of larger cars, but it was not long before the love of luxury and the tendency to spend conspicuously, which characterizes the American people, reasserted themselves, and this, when reenforced by a growing belief in the greater safety of bigger cars, was soon reflected in a relative decline in consumer demand for small cars (other than sport models) by all but the most economically minded.

APPENDIXES

PLESSY v. FERGUSON

163 U.S. 537
16 S.Ct. 1138
41 L.Ed. 256

STATEMENT OF THE CASE

This was a petition for writs of prohibition and certiorari, originally filed in the Supreme Court of the State by Plessy, the plaintiff in error, against the Hon. John H. Ferguson, judge of the criminal District Court for the parish of Orleans, and setting forth in substance the following facts:

That petitioner was a citizen of the United States and a resident of the State of Louisiana, of mixed descent, in the proportion of seven eighths Caucasian and one eighth African blood; that the mixture of colored blood was not discernible in him, and that he was entitled to every recognition, right, privilege and immunity secured to the citizens of the United States of the white race by its Constitution and laws; that on June 7, 1892, he engaged and paid for a first class passage on the East Louisiana Railway from New Orleans to Covington, in the same State, and thereupon entered a passenger train, and took possession of a vacant seat in a coach where passengers of the white race were accommodated; that such railroad company was incorporated by the laws of Louisiana as a common carrier, and was not authorized to distinguish between citizens according to their race. But, notwithstanding this, petitioner was required by the conductor, under penalty of ejection from said train and imprisonment, to vacate said coach and occupy another seat in a coach assigned by said company for persons not of the white race, and for no other reason than that petitioner was of the colored race; that upon petitioner's refusal to comply with such order, he was, with the aid of a police officer, forcibly ejected from said coach and hurried off to and imprisoned in the parish jail of New Orleans, and there held to answer a charge made by such officer to the effect that he was guilty of having criminally violated an act of the General Assembly of the State, approved July 10, 1890, in such case made and provided.

That petitioner was subsequently brought before the recorder of the city for preliminary examination and committed for trial to the criminal District Court for the parish of Orleans, where an information was filed against him in the matter above set forth, for a violation of the above act, which act the petitioner affirmed to be null and void, because in conflict with the Constitution of the United States; that petitioner interposed a plea to such information, based upon the unconstitutionality of the act of the General Assembly, to which the district attorney, on behalf of the State, filed a demurrer; that, upon issue being joined upon such demurrer and plea, the court sustained the demurrer, overruled the plea, and ordered petitioner to plead over to the facts set forth in the information, and that, unless the judge of the said court be enjoined by a writ of prohibition from further proceeding in such case, the court will proceed to fine and sentence petitioner to imprisonment, and thus deprive him of his constitutional rights set forth in his said plea, notwithstanding the unconstitutionality of the act under which he was being prosecuted; that no appeal lay from such sentence, and petitioner was without relief or remedy except by writs of prohibition and certiorari. Copies of the information and other proceedings in the criminal District Court were annexed to the petition as an exhibit.

Upon the filing of this petition, an order was issued upon the respondent to show cause why a writ of prohibition should not issue and be made perpetual, and a further order that the record of the proceedings had in the criminal cause be certified and transmitted to the Supreme Court.

To this order the respondent made answer, transmitting a certified copy of the proceedings, asserting the constitutionality of the law, and averring that, instead of pleading or admitting that he belonged to the colored race, the said Plessy declined and refused, either by pleading or otherwise, to admit that he was in any sense or in any proportion a colored man.

The case coming on for a hearing before the Supreme Court, that court was of opinion that the law under which the prosecution was had was constitutional, and denied the relief prayed for by the petitioner. *Ex parte Plessy*, 45 La. Ann. 80. Whereupon petitioner prayed for a writ of error from this court which was allowed by the Chief Justice of the Supreme Court of Louisiana.

OPINION OF THE COURT

This case turns upon the constitutionality of an act of the General Assembly of the State of Louisiana, passed in 1890, providing for separate railway carriages for the white and colored races. Acts 1890, No. 111, p. 152.

The first section of the statute enacts "that all railway companies carrying passengers in their coaches in this State, shall provide equal but separate accommodations for the white, and colored races, by providing two or more passenger coaches for each passenger train, or by dividing the passenger coaches by a partition so as to secure separate accommodations: *Provided*, That this section shall not be construed to apply to street railroads. No person or persons, shall be admitted to occupy seats in coaches, other than, the ones, assigned, to them on account of the race they belong to."

By the second section it was enacted "that the officers of such passenger trains shall have power and are hereby required to assign each passenger to the coach or compartment used for the race to which such passenger belongs; any passenger insisting on going into a coach or compartment to which by race he does not belong, shall be liable to a fine of twenty-five dollars, or in lieu thereof to imprisonment for a period of not more than twenty days in the parish prison, and any officer of any railroad insisting on assigning a passenger to a coach or compartment other than the one set aside for the race to which said passenger belongs, shall be liable to a fine of twenty-five dollars, or in lieu thereof to imprisonment for a period of not more than twenty days in the parish prison; and should any passenger refuse to occupy the coach or compartment to which he or she is assigned by the officer of such railway, said officer shall have power to refuse to carry such passenger on his train, and for such refusal neither he nor the railway company which he represents shall be liable for damages in any of the courts of this State."

The third section provides penalties for the refusal or neglect of the officers, directors, conductors and employes of railway companies to comply with the act, with a proviso that "nothing in this act shall be construed as applying to nurses attending children of the other race." The fourth section is immaterial.

The information filed in the criminal District Court charged in substance that Plessy, being a passenger between two stations within the State of Louisiana, was assigned by officers of the company to the coach used for the race to which he belonged, but he insisted upon going into a coach used by the race to which he did not belong. Neither in the information nor plea was his particular race or color averred.

The petition for the writ of prohibition averred that petitioner was seven eighths Caucasian and one eighth African blood; that the mixture of colored blood was not discernible in him, and that he was entitled to every right, privilege and immunity secured to citizens of the United States of the white race; and that, upon such theory, he took possession of a vacant seat in a coach where passengers of the white race were accommodated, and was ordered by the conductor to vacate said coach and take a seat in another assigned to persons of the colored race, and having refused to comply with such demand he was forcibly ejected with the aid of a police officer, and imprisoned in the parish jail to answer a charge of having violated the above act.

The constitutionality of this act is attacked upon the ground that it conflicts both with the Thirteenth Amendment of the Constitution, abolishing slavery, and the Fourteenth Amendment, which prohibits certain restrictive legislation on the part of the States.

1. That it does not conflict with the Thirteenth Amendment, which abolished slavery and involuntary servitude, except as a punishment for crime, is too clear for argument. Slavery implies involuntary servitude—a state of bondage; the ownership of mankind as a chattel, or at least the control of the labor and services of one man for the benefit of another, and the absence of a legal right to the disposal of his own person, property and services. This amendment was said in the *Slaughter-house cases*, 16 Wall. 36, to have been intended primarily to abolish slavery, as it had been previously known in this country, and that it equally forbade Mexican peonage or the Chinese coolie trade, when they amounted to slavery or involuntary servitude, and that the use of the word "servitude" was intended to prohibit the use of all forms of involuntary slavery, of whatever class or name. It was intimated, however, in that case that this amendment was regarded by the statesmen of that day as insufficient to protect the colored race from certain laws

which had been enacted in the Southern States, imposing upon the colored race onerous disabilities and burdens, and curtailing their rights in the pursuit of life, liberty and property to such an extent that their freedom was of little value; and that the Fourteenth Amendment was devised to meet this exigency.

So, too, in the *Civil Rights cases*, 109 U. S. 3, 24, it was said that the act of a mere individual, the owner of an inn, a public conveyance or place of amusement, refusing accommodations to colored people, cannot be justly regarded as imposing any badge of slavery or servitude upon the applicant, but only as involving an ordinary civil injury, properly cognizable by the laws of the State, and presumably subject to redress by those laws until the contrary appears. "It would be running the slavery argument into the ground," said Mr. Justice Bradley, "to make it apply to every act of discrimination which a person may see fit to make as to the guests he will entertain, or as to the people he will take into his coach or cab or car, or admit to his concert or theatre, or deal with in other matters of intercourse or business."

A statute which implies merely a legal distinction between the white and colored races—a distinction which is founded in the color of the two races, and which must always exist so long as white men are distinguished from the other race by color—has no tendency to destroy the legal equality of the two races, or reëstablish a state of involuntary servitude. Indeed, we do not understand that the Thirteenth Amendment is strenuously relied upon by the plaintiff in error in this connection.

2. By the Fourteenth Amendment, all persons born or naturalized in the United States, and subject to the jurisdiction thereof, are made citizens of the United States and of the State wherein they reside; and the States are forbid-

den from making or enforcing any law which shall abridge the privileges or immunities of citizens of the United States, or shall deprive any person of life, liberty or property without due process of law, or deny to any person within their jurisdiction the equal protection of the laws.

The proper construction of this amendment was first called to the attention of this court in the *Slaughter-house cases*, 16 Wall. 36, which involved, however, not a question of race, but one of exclusive privileges. The case did not call for any expression of opinion as to the exact rights it was intended to secure to the colored race, but it was said generally that its main purpose was to establish the citizenship of the negro; to give definitions of citizenship of the United States and of the States, and to protect from the hostile legislation of the States the privileges and immunities of citizens of the United States, as distinguished from those of citizens of the States.

The object of the amendment was undoubtedly to enforce the absolute equality of the two races before the law, but in the nature of things it could not have been intended to abolish distinctions based upon color, or to enforce social, as distinguished from political equality, or a commingling of the two races upon terms unsatisfactory to either. Laws permitting, and even requiring, their separation in places where they are liable to be brought into contact do not necessarily imply the inferiority of either race to the other, and have been generally, if not universally, recognized as within the competency of the state legislatures in the exercise of their police power. The most common instance of this is connected with the establishment of separate schools for white and colored children, which has been held to be a valid exercise of the legislative power even by courts of States where the political rights of the colored race have been longest and most earnestly enforced.

One of the earliest of these cases is that of *Roberts* v. *City of Boston*, 5 Cush. 198, in which the Supreme Judicial Court of Massachusetts held that the general school committee of Boston had power to make provision for the instruction of colored children in separate schools established exclusively for them, and to prohibit their attendance upon the other schools. "The great principle," said Chief Justice Shaw, p. 206, "advanced by the learned and eloquent advocate for the plaintiff," (Mr. Charles Sumner,) "is, that by the constitution and laws of Massachusetts, all persons without distinction of age or sex, birth or color, origin or condition, are equal before the law. . . . But, when this great principle comes to be applied to the actual and various conditions of persons in society, it will not warrant the assertion, that men and women are legally clothed with the same civil and political powers, and that children and adults are legally to have the same functions and be subject to the same treatment; but only that the rights of all, as they are settled and regulated by law, are equally entitled to the paternal consideration and protection of the law for their maintenance and security." It was held that the powers of the committee extended to the establishment of separate schools for children of different ages, sexes and colors, and that they might also establish schools for poor and neglected children, who have become too old to attend the primary school, and yet have not acquired the rudiments of learning, to enable them to enter the ordinary schools. Similar laws have been enacted by Congress under its general power of legislation over the District of Columbia, Rev. Stat. D. C. §§281, 282, 283, 310, 319, as well as by the legislatures of many of the States, and have been generally, if not uniformly, sustained by the courts. *State* v. *McCann*, 21 Ohio St. 198; *Lehew* v. *Brummell*, 15 S. W. Rep. 765; *Ward* v. *Flood*, 48 California, 36; *Bertonneau v. School Directors*, 3 Woods, 177; *People* v.

Gallagher, 93 N. Y. 438; *Cory* v. *Carter*, 48 Indiana, 327; *Dawson* v. *Lee*, 83 Kentucky, 49.

Laws forbidding the intermarriage of the two races may be said in a technical sense to interfere with the freedom of contract, and yet have been universally recognized as within the police power of the State. *State* v. *Gibson*, 36 Indiana, 389.

The distinction between laws interfering with the political equality of the negro and those requiring the separation of the two races in schools, theatres and railway carriages has been frequently drawn by this court. Thus in *Strauder* v. *West Virginia*, 100 U. S. 303, it was held that a law of West Virginia limiting to white male persons, 21 years of age and citizens of the State, the right to sit upon juries, was a discrimination which implied a legal inferiority in civil society, which lessened the security of the right of the colored race, and was a step toward reducing them to a condition of servility. Indeed, the right of a colored man that, in the selection of jurors to pass upon his life, liberty and property, there shall be no exclusion of his race, and no discrimination against them because of color, has been asserted in a number of cases. *Virginia* v. *Rives*, 100 U. S. 313; *Neal* v. *Delaware*, 103 U. S. 370; *Bush* v. *Kentucky*, 107 U. S. 110; *Gibson* v. *Mississippi*, 162 U. S. 565. So, where the laws of a particular locality or the charter of a particular railway corporation has provided that no person shall be excluded from the cars on account of color, we have held that this meant that persons of color should travel in the same car as white ones, and that the enactment was not satisfied by the company's providing cars assigned exclusively to people of color, though they were as good as those which they assigned exclusively to white persons. *Railroad Company* v. *Brown*, 17 Wall. 445.

Upon the other hand, where a statute of Louisiana required those engaged in the transportation of passengers among the States to give to all persons travelling within that State, upon vessels employed in that business, equal rights and privileges in all parts of the vessel, without distinction on account of race or color, and subjected to an action for damages the owner of such a vessel, who excluded colored passengers on account of their color from the cabin set aside by him for the use of whites, it was held to be so far as it applied to interstate commerce, unconstitutional and void. *Hall* v. *De Cuir*, 95 U. S. 485. The court in this case, however, expressly disclaimed that it had anything whatever to do with the statute as a regulation of internal commerce, or affecting anything else than commerce among the States.

In the *Civil Rights case*, 109 U. S. 3, it was held that an act of Congress, entitling all persons within the jurisdiction of the United States to the full and equal enjoyment of the accommodations, advantages, facilities and privileges of inns, public conveyances, on land or water, theatres and other places of public amusement, and made applicable to citizens of every race and color, regardless of any previous condition of servitude, was unconstitutional and void, upon the ground that the Fourteenth Amendment was prohibitory upon the States only, and the legislation authorized to be adopted by Congress for enforcing it was not direct legislation on matters respecting which the States were prohibited from making or enforcing certain laws, or doing certain acts, but was corrective legislation, such as might be necessary or proper for counteracting and redressing the effect of such laws or acts. In delivering the opinion of the court Mr. Justice Bradley observed that the Fourteenth Amendment "does not invest Congress with power to legislate upon subjects that are within the domain of state legislation; but to provide modes of relief against state legislation, or state action, of the kind referred to. It does not authorize Congress to create a code of municipal law for the regulation of private rights; but to provide modes of redress against the operation of state laws, and the action of state officers, executive or judicial, when these are subversive of the fundamental rights specified in the amendment. Positive rights and privileges are undoubtedly secured by the Fourteenth Amendment; but they are secured by way of prohibition against state laws and state proceedings affecting those rights and privileges, and by power given to Congress to legislate for the purpose of carrying such prohibition into effect; and such legislation must necessarily be predicated upon such supposed state laws or state proceedings, and be directed to the correction of their operation and effect."

Much nearer, and, indeed, almost directly in point, is the case of the *Louisville, New Orleans &c. Railway* v. *Mississippi*, 133 U. S. 587, wherein the railway company was indicted for a violation of a statute of Mississippi, enacting that all railroads carrying passengers should provide equal, but separate, accommodations for the white and colored races, by providing two or more passenger cars for each passenger train, or by dividing the passenger cars by a partition, so as to secure separate accommodations. The case was presented in a different aspect from the one under consideration, inasmuch as it was an indictment against the railway company for failing to provide the separate accommodations, but the question considered was the constitutionality of the law. In that case, the Supreme Court of Mississippi, 66 Mississippi, 662, had held that the statute applied solely to commerce within the State, and, that being the construction of the state statute by its highest court, was accepted as conclusive. "If it be a matter," said the court, p. 591, "respecting commerce wholly within a State, and not interfering with commerce between the States, then, obviously, there is no violation of the commerce clause of the Federal Constitution. . . . No question arises under this section, as to the power of the State to separate in different compartments interstate passengers, or affect, in any manner, the privileges and rights of such passengers. All that we can consider is, whether the State has the power to require that railroad trains within her limits shall have separate accommodations for the two races; that affecting only commerce within the State is no invasion of the power given to Congress by the commerce clause."

A like course of reasoning applies to the case under consideration, since the Supreme Court of Louisiana in the case of the *State ex rel. Abbott* v. *Hicks, Judge, et al.*, 44 La. Ann. 770, held that the statute in question did not apply to interstate passengers, but was confined in its application to passengers travelling exclusively within the borders of the State. The case was decided largely upon the authority of *Railway Co.* v. *State*, 66 Mississippi, 662, and affirmed by this court in 133 U. S. 587. In the present case no question of interference with interstate commerce can possibly arise, since the East Louisiana Railway appears to have been purely a local line, with both its termini within the State of Louisiana. Similar statutes for the separation of the two races upon public conveyances were held to be constitutional in *West Chester &c. Railroad* v. *Miles*, 55 Penn. St. 209; *Day* v. *Owen*, 5 Michigan, 520; *Chicago &c. Railway* v. *Williams*, 55 Illinois, 185; *Chesapeake &c. Railroad* v. *Wells*, 85 Tennessee, 613; *Memphis &c. Railroad* v. *Benson*, 85 Tennessee, 627; *The Sue*, 22 Fed. Rep. 843; *Logwood* v. *Memphis &c. Railroad*, 23 Fed. Rep. 318; *McGuinn* v. *Forbes*, 37 Fed. Rep. 639; *People* v. *King*, 18 N. E. Rep. 245; *Houck* v. *South Pac. Railway*, 38 Fed. Rep. 226; *Heard* v. *Georgia Railroad Co.*, 3 Int. Com. Com'n, 111; *S. C.*, 1 Ibid. 428.

While we think the enforced separation of the races, as applied to the internal commerce of the State, neither abridges the privileges or immunities of the colored man, deprives him of his property without due process of law, nor denies him the equal protection of the laws, within the meaning of the Fourteenth Amendment, we are not prepared to say that the conductor, in assigning passengers to the coaches according to their race, does not act at his peril, or that the provision of the second section of the act, that denies to the passenger compensation in damages for a refusal to receive him into the coach in which he properly belongs, is a valid exercise of the legislative power. Indeed, we understand it to be conceded by the State's attorney, that such part of the act as exempts from liability the railway company and its officers is unconstitutional. The power to assign to a particular coach obviously implies the power to determine to which race the passenger belongs, as well as the power to determine who, under the laws of the particular State, is to be deemed a white, and who a colored person. This question, though indicated in the brief of the plaintiff in error, does not properly arise upon the record in this case, since the only issue made is as to the unconstitutionality of the act, so far as it requires the railway to provide separate accommodations, and the conductor to assign passengers according to their race.

It is claimed by the plaintiff in error that, in any mixed community, the reputation of belonging to the dominant race, in this instance the white race, is *property*, in the same sense that a right of action, or of inheritance, is property. Conceding this to be so, for the purposes of this case, we are unable to see how this statute deprives him of, or in any way affects his right to, such property. If he be a white man and assigned to a colored coach, he may have his action for damages against the company for being deprived of his so called property. Upon the other hand, if he be a colored man and be so assigned, he has been deprived of no property, since he is not lawfully entitled to the reputation of being a white man.

In this connection, it is also suggested by the learned counsel for the plaintiff in error that the same argument that will justify the state legislature in requiring railways to provide separate accommodations for the two races will also authorize them to require separate cars to be provided for people whose hair is of a certain color, or who are aliens, or who belong to certain nationalities, or to enact laws requiring colored people to walk upon one side of the street, and white people upon the other, or requiring white men's houses to be painted white, and colored men's black, or their vehicles or business signs to be of different colors, upon the theory that one side of the street is as good as the other, or that a house or vehicle of one color is as good as one of another color. The reply to all this is that every exercise of the police power must be reasonable, and extend only to such laws as are enacted in good faith for the promotion for the public good, and not for the annoyance or oppression of a particular class. Thus in *Yick Wo* v. *Hopkins*, 118 U. S. 356, it was held by this court that a municipal ordinance of the city of San Francisco, to regulate the carrying on of public laundries within the limits of the municipality, violated the provisions of the Constitution of the United States, if it conferred upon the municipal authorities arbitrary power, at their own will, and without regard to discretion, in the legal sense of the term, to give or withhold consent as to persons or places, without regard to the competency of the persons applying, or the propriety of the places selected for the carrying on of the business. It was held to be a covert attempt on the part of the municipality to make an arbitrary and unjust discrimination against the Chinese race. While this was the case of a municipal ordinance, a like principle has been held to apply to acts of a state legislature passed in the exercise of the police power. *Railroad Company* v. *Husen*, 95 U. S. 465; *Louisville & Nashville Railroad* v. *Kentucky*, 161 U. S. 677, and cases cited on p. 700; *Daggett* v. *Hudson*, 43 Ohio St. 548; *Capen* v. *Foster*, 12 Pick. 485; *State ex rel. Wood* v. *Baker*, 38 Wisconsin, 71; *Monroe* v. *Collins*, 17 Ohio St. 665; *Hulseman* v. *Rems*, 41 Penn. St. 396; *Orman* v. *Riley*, 15 California, 48.

So far, then, as a conflict with the Fourteenth Amendment is concerned, the case reduces itself to the question whether the statute of Louisiana is a reasonable regulation, and with respect to this there must necessarily be a large discretion on the part of the legislature. In determining the question of reasonableness it is at liberty to act with reference to the established usages, customs and traditions of the people, and with a view to the promotion of their comfort, and the preservation of the public peace and good order. Gauged by this standard, we cannot say that a law which authorizes or even requires the separation of the two races in public conveyances is unreasonable, or more obnoxious to the Fourteenth Amendment than the acts of Congress requiring separate schools for colored children in the District of Columbia, the constitutionality of which does not seem to have been questioned, or the corresponding acts of state legislatures.

We consider the underlying fallacy of the plaintiff's argument to consist in the assumption that the enforced separation of the two races stamps the colored race with a badge of inferiority. If this be so, it is not by reason of anything found in the act, but solely because the colored race chooses to put that construction upon it. The argument necessarily assumes that if, as has been more than once the case, and is not unlikely to be so again, the colored race should become the dominant power in the state legislature, and should enact a law in precisely similar terms, it would thereby regulate the white race to an inferior position. We imagine that the white race, at least, would not acquiesce in this assumption. The argument also assumes that social prejudices may be overcome by legislation, and that equal rights cannot be secured to the negro except by an enforced commingling of the two races. We cannot accept this proposition. If the two races are to meet upon terms of social equality, it must be the result of natural affinities, a mutual appreciation of each other's merits and a voluntary consent of individuals. As was said by the Court of Appeals of New York in *People* v. *Gallagher*, 93 N. Y. 438, 448, "this end can neither be accomplished nor promoted by laws which conflict with the general sentiment of the community upon whom they are designed to operate. When the government, therefore, has secured to each of its citizens equal rights before the law and equal opportunities for improvement and progress, it has accomplished the end for which it was organized and performed all of the functions respecting social advantages with which it is endowed." Legislation is powerless to eradicate racial instincts or to abolish distinctions based upon physical differences, and the attempt to do so can only result in accentuating the difficulties of the present situation. If the civil and political rights of both races be equal one cannot be inferior to the other civilly or politically. If one race be inferior to the other socially, the Constitution of the United States cannot put them upon the same plane.

It is true that the question of the proportion of colored blood necessary to constitute a colored person, as distinguished from a white person, is one upon which there is a difference of opinion in the different States, some holding that any visible admixture of black blood stamps the person as belonging to the colored race, (*State* v. *Chavers*, 5 Jones, [N. C.] 1, p. 11); others that it depends upon the preponderance of blood, (*Gray* v. *State*, 4 Ohio, 354; *Monroe* v. *Collins*, 17 Ohio St. 665); and still others that the predominance of white blood must only be in the proportion of three fourths. (*People* v. *Dean*, 14 Michigan, 406; *Jones* v. *Commonwealth*, 80 Virginia, 538.) But these are questions to be determined under the laws of each State and are not properly put in issue in this case. Under the allegations of his petition it may undoubtedly become a question of importance whether, under the laws of Louisiana, the petitioner belongs to the white or colored race.

The judgment of the court below is, therefore,

Affirmed.

MR. JUSTICE HARLAN dissenting.

JUSTICE HARLAN'S DISSENTING OPINION

By the Louisiana statute, the validity of which is here involved, all railway companies (other than street railroad companies) carrying passengers in that State are required to have separate but equal accommodations for white and colored persons, "by providing two or more passenger coaches for each passenger train, *or* by dividing the passenger coaches by a *partition* so as to secure separate accommodations." Under this statute, no colored person is permitted to occupy a seat in a coach assigned to white persons; nor any white person, to occupy a seat in a coach assigned to colored persons. The managers of the railroad are not allowed to exercise any discretion in the premises, but are required to assign each passenger to some coach or compartment set apart for the exclusive use of his race. If a passenger insists upon going into a coach or compartment not set apart for persons of his race, he is subject to be fined, or to be imprisoned in the parish jail. Penalties are prescribed for the refusal or neglect of the officers, directors, conductors and employes of railroad companies to comply with the provisions of the act.

Only "nurses attending children of the other race" are excepted from the operation of the statute. No exception is made of colored attendants travelling with adults. A white man is not permitted to have his colored servant with him in the same coach, even if his condition of health requires the constant, personal assistance of such servant. If a colored maid insists upon riding in the same coach with a white woman whom she has been employed to serve, and who may need her personal attention while travelling, she is subject to be fined or imprisoned for such an exhibition of zeal in the discharge of duty.

While there may be in Louisiana persons of different races who are not citizens of the United States, the words in the act, "white and colored races," necessarily include all citizens of the United States of both races residing in that State. So that we have before us a state enactment that compels, under penalties, the separation of the two races in railroad passenger coaches, and makes it a crime for a citizen of either race to enter a coach that has been assigned to citizens of the other race.

Thus the State regulates the use of a public highway by citizens of the United States solely upon the basis of race.

However apparent the injustice of such legislation may be, we have only to consider whether it is consistent with the Constitution of the United States.

That a railroad is a public highway, and that the corporation which owns or operates it is in the exercise of public functions, is not, at this day, to be disputed. Mr. Justice Nelson, speaking for this court in *New Jersey Steam Navigation Co.* v. *Merchants' Bank*, 6 How. 344, 382, said that a common carrier was in the exercise "of a sort of public office, and has public duties to perform, from which he should not be permitted to exonerate himself without the assent of the parties concerned." Mr. Justice Strong, delivering the judgment of this court in *Olcott* v. *The Supervisors*, 16 Wall. 678, 694, said: "That railroads, though constructed by private corporations and owned by them, are public highways, has been the doctrine of nearly all the courts ever since such conveniences for passage and transportation have had any existence. Very early the question arose whether a State's right of eminent domain could be exercised by a private corporation created for the purpose of constructing a railroad. Clearly it could not, unless taking land for such a purpose by such an agency is taking land for public use. The right of eminent domain nowhere justifies taking property for a private use. Yet it is a doctrine universally accepted that a state legislature may authorize a private corporation to take land for the construction of such a road, making compensation to the owner. What else does this doctrine mean if not that building a railroad, though it be built by a private corporation, is an act done for a public use?" So, in *Township of Pine Grove* v. *Talcott*, 19 Wall. 666, 676: "Though the corporation [a railroad company] was private, its work was public, as much so as if it were to be constructed by the State." So, in *Inhabitants of Worcester* v. *Western Railroad Corporation*, 4 Met. 564: "The establishment of that great thoroughfare is regarded as a public work, established by public authority, intended for the public use and benefit, the use of which is secured to the whole community, and constitutes, therefore, like a canal, turnpike or highway, a public easement. It is true that the real and personal property, necessary to the establishment of the railroad, is vested in the corporation; but it is in trust for the public."

In respect of civil rights, common to all citizens, the Constitution of the United States does not, I think, permit any public authority to know the race of those entitled to be protected in the enjoyment of such rights. Every true man has pride of race, and under appropriate circumstances when the rights of others, his equals before the law, are not to be affected, it is his privilege to express such pride and to take such action based upon it as to him seems proper. But I deny that any legislative body or judicial tribunal may have regard to the race of citizens when the civil rights of those citizens are involved. Indeed, such legislation, as that here in question, is inconsistent not only with that equality of rights which pertains to citizenship, National and State, but with the personal liberty enjoyed by every one within the United States.

The Thirteenth Amendment does not permit the withholding or the deprivation of any right necessarily inhering in freedom. It not only struck down the institution of slavery as previously existing in the United States, but it prevents the imposition of any burdens or disabilities that constitute badges of slavery or servitude. It decreed universal civil freedom in this country. This court has so adjudged. But that amendment having been found inadequate to the protection of the rights of those who had been in slavery, it was followed by the Fourteenth Amendment, which added greatly to the dignity and glory of American citizenship, and to the security of personal liberty, by declaring that "all persons born or naturalized in the United States, and subject to the jurisdiction thereof, are citizens of the United States and of the State wherein they reside," and that "no State shall make or enforce any law which shall abridge the privileges or immunities of citizens of the United States; nor shall any State deprive any person of life, liberty or property without due process of law, nor deny to any person within its jurisdiction the equal protection of the laws." These two amendments, if enforced according to their true intent and meaning, will protect all the civil rights that pertain to freedom and citizenship. Finally, and to the end that no citizen should be denied, on account of his race, the privilege of participating in the political control of his country, it was declared by the Fifteenth Amendment that "the right of citizens of the United States to vote shall not be denied or abridged by the United States or by any State on account of race, color or previous condition of servitude."

These notable additions to the fundamental law were welcomed by the friends of liberty throughout the world. They removed the race line from our governmental systems. They had, as this court has said, a common purpose, namely, to secure "to a race recently emancipated, a race that through many generations have been held in slavery, all the civil rights that the superior race enjoy." They declared, in legal effect, this court has further said, "that the law in the States shall be the same for the black as for the white; that all persons, whether colored or white, shall stand equal before the laws of the States, and, in regard to the colored race, for whose protection the amendment was primarily designed, that no discrimination shall be made against them by law because of their color." We also said: "The words of the amendment, it is true, are prohibitory, but they contain a necessary implication of a positive immunity, or right, most valuable to the colored race—the right to exemption from unfriendly legislation against them distinctively as colored—exemption from legal discriminations, implying inferiority in civil society, lessening the security of their enjoyment of the rights which others enjoy, and discriminations which are steps towards reducing them to the condition of a subject race." It was, consequently, adjudged that a state law that excluded citizens of the colored race from juries, because of their race and however well qualified in other respects to discharge the duties of jurymen, was repugnant to the Fourteenth Amendment. *Strauder* v. *West Virginia,* 100 U. S. 303, 306, 307; *Virginia* v. *Rives,* 100 U. S. 313; *Ex parte Virginia,* 100 U. S. 339; *Neal* v. *Delaware,* 103 U. S. 370, 386; *Bush* v. *Kentucky,* 107 U. S. 110, 116. At the present term, referring to the previous adjudications, this court declared that "underlying all of those decisions is the principle that the Constitution of the United States, in its present form, forbids, so far as civil and political rights are concerned, discrimination by the General Government or the States against any citizen because of his race. All citizens are equal before the law." *Gibson* v. *Mississippi,* 162 U. S. 565.

The decisions referred to show the scope of the recent amendments of the Constitution. They also show that it is not within the power of a State to prohibit colored citizens, because of their race, from participating as jurors in the administration of justice.

It was said in argument that the statute of Louisiana does not discriminate against either race, but prescribes a rule applicable alike to white and colored citizens. But this argument does not meet the difficulty. Every one knows that the statute in question had its origin in the purpose, not so much to exclude white persons from railroad cars occupied by blacks, as to exclude colored people from coaches occupied by or assigned to white persons. Railroad corporations of Louisiana did not make discrimination among whites in the matter of accommodation for travellers. The thing to accomplish was, under the guise of giving equal accommodation for whites and blacks, to compel the latter to keep to themselves while travelling in railroad passenger coaches. No one would be so wanting in candor as to assert the contrary. The fundamental objection, therefore, to the statute is that it interferes with the personal freedom of citizens. "Personal liberty," it has been well said, "consists in the power of locomotion, of changing situation, or removing one's person to whatsoever places one's own inclination may direct, without imprisonment or restraint, unless by due course of law." 1 Bl. Com. *134. If a white man and a black man choose to occupy the same public conveyance on a public highway, it is their right to do so, and no government, proceeding alone on grounds of race, can prevent it without infringing the personal liberty of each.

It is one thing for railroad carriers to furnish, or to be required by law to furnish, equal accommodations for all whom they are under a legal duty to carry. It is quite another thing for government to forbid citizens of the white and black races from travelling in the same public conveyance, and to punish officers of railroad companies for permitting persons of the two races to occupy the same passenger coach. If a State can prescribe, as a rule of civil conduct, that whites and blacks shall not travel as passengers in the same railroad coach, why may it not so regulate the use of the streets of its cities and towns as to compel white citizens to keep on one side of a street and black citizens to keep on the other? Why may it not, upon like grounds, punish whites and blacks who ride together in street cars or in open vehicles on a public road or street? Why may it not require sheriffs to assign whites to one side of a court-room and blacks to the other? And why may it not also prohibit the commingling of the two races in the galleries of legislative halls or in public assemblages convened for the consideration of the political questions of the day? Further, if this statute of Louisiana is consistent with the personal liberty of citizens, why may not the State require the separation in railroad coaches of native and naturalized citizens of the United States, or of Protestants and Roman Catholics?

The answer given at the argument to these questions was that regulations of the kind they suggest would be unreasonable, and could not, therefore, stand before the law. Is it meant that the determination of questions of legislative power depends upon the inquiry whether the statute whose validity is questioned is, in the judgment of the courts, a reasonable one, taking all the circumstances into consideration? A statute may be unreasonable merely because a sound public policy forbade its enactment. But I do not understand that the courts have anything to do with the policy or expediency of legislation. A statute may be valid, and yet, upon grounds of public policy, may well be characterized as unreasonable. Mr. Sedgwick correctly states the rule when he says that the legislative intention being clearly ascertained, "the courts have no other duty to perform than to execute the legislative will, without any regard to their views as to the wisdom or justice of the particular enactment." Stat. & Const. Constr. 324. There is a dangerous tendency in these latter days to enlarge the functions of the courts, by means of judicial interference with the will of the people as expressed by the legislature. Our institutions have the distinguishing characteristic that the three departments of government are coördinate and separate. Each must keep within the limits defined by the Constitution. And the courts best discharge their duty by executing the will of the law-making power, constitutionally expressed, leaving the results of legislation to be dealt with by the people through their representatives. Statutes must always have a reasonable construction. Sometimes they are to be construed strictly; sometimes, liberally, in order to carry out the legislative will. But however construed, the intent of the legislature is to be respected, if the particular statute in question is valid, although the courts, looking at the public interests, may conceive the statute to be both unreasonable and impolitic. If the power exists to enact a statute, that ends the matter so far as the courts are concerned. The adjudged cases in which statutes have been held to be void, because unreasonable, are those in which the means employed by the legislature were not at all germane to the end to which the legislature was competent.

The white race deems itself to be the dominant race in this country. And so it is, in prestige, in achievements, in education, in wealth and in power. So, I doubt not, it will continue to be for all time, if it remains true to its great heritage and holds fast to the principles of constitutional liberty. But in view of the Constitution, in the eye of the law, there is in this country no superior, dominant, ruling class of citizens. There is no caste here. Our Constitution is color-blind, and neither knows nor tolerates classes among citizens. In respect of civil rights, all citizens are equal before the law. The humblest is the peer of the most powerful. The law regards man as man, and takes no account of his surroundings or of his color when his civil rights as guaranteed by the supreme law of the land are involved. It is, therefore, to be regretted that this high tribunal, the final expositor of the fundamental law of the land, has reached the conclusion that it is competent for a State to regulate the enjoyment by citizens of their civil rights solely upon the basis of race.

In my opinion, the judgment this day rendered will, in time, prove to be quite as pernicious as the decision made by this tribunal in the *Dred Scott case*. It was adjudged in that case that the descendants of Africans who were imported into this country and sold as slaves were not included nor intended to be included under the word "citizens" in the Constitution, and could not claim any of the rights and privileges which that instrument provided for and secured to citizens of the United States; that at the time of the adoption of the Constitution they were "considered as a subordinate and inferior class of beings, who had been subjugated by the dominant race, and, whether emancipated or not, yet remained subject to their authority, and had no rights or privileges but such as those who held the power and the government might choose to grant them." 19 How. 393, 404. The recent amendments of the Constitution, it was supposed, had eradicated these principles from our institutions. But it seems that we have yet, in some of the States, a dominant race—a superior class of citizens, which assumes to regulate the enjoyment of civil rights, common to all citizens, upon the basis of race. The present decision, it may well be apprehended, will not only stimulate aggressions, more or less brutal and irritating, upon the admitted rights of colored citizens, but will encourage the belief that it is possible, by means of state enactments, to defeat the beneficent purposes which the people of the United States had in view when they adopted the recent amendments of the Constitution, by one of which the blacks of this country were made citizens of the United States and of the States in which they respectively reside, and whose privileges and immunities, as citizens, the States are forbidden to abridge. Sixty millions of whites are in no danger from the presence here of eight millions of blacks. The destinies of the two races, in this country, are indissolubly linked together, and the interests of both require that the common government of all shall not permit the seeds of race hate to be planted under the sanction of law. What can more certainly arouse race hate, what more certainly create and perpetuate a feeling of distrust between these races, than state enactments, which, in fact, proceed on the ground that colored citizens are so inferior and degraded that they cannot be allowed to sit in public coaches occupied by white citizens? That, as all will admit, is the real meaning of such legislation as was enacted in Louisiana.

The sure guarantee of the peace and security of each race is the clear, distinct, unconditional recognition by our governments, National and State, of every right that inheres in civil freedom, and of the equality before the law of all citizens of the United States without regard to race. State enactments, regulating the enjoyment of civil rights, upon the basis of race, and cunningly devised to defeat legitimate results of the war, under the pretence of recognizing equality of rights, can have no other result than to render permanent peace impossible, and to keep alive a conflict of races, the continuance of which must do harm to all concerned. This question is not met by the suggestion that social equality cannot exist between the white and black races in this country. That argument, if it can be properly regarded as one, is scarcely worthy of consideration; for social equality no more exists between two races when travelling in a passenger coach or a public highway than when members of the same races sit by each other in a street car or in the jury box, or stand or sit with each other in a political assembly, or when they use in common the streets of a city or town, or when they are in the same room for the purpose of having their names placed on the registry of voters, or when they approach the ballot-box in order to exercise the high privilege of voting.

There is a race so different from our own that we do not permit those belonging to it to become citizens of the United States. Persons belonging to it are, with few exceptions, absolutely excluded from our country. I allude to the Chinese race. But by the statute in question, a Chinaman can ride in the same passenger coach with white citizens of the United States, while citizens of the black race in Louisiana, many of whom, perhaps, risked their lives for the preservation of the Union, who are entitled, by law, to participate in the political control of the State and nation, who are not excluded, by law or by reason of their race, from public stations of any kind, and who have all the legal rights that belong to white citizens, are yet declared to be criminals, liable to imprisonment, if they ride in a public coach occupied by citizens of the white race. It is scarcely just to say that a colored citizen should not object to occupying a public coach assigned to his own race. He does not object, nor, perhaps, would he object to separate coaches for his race, if his rights under the law were recognized. But he objects, and ought never to cease objecting to the proposition, that citizens of the white and black races can be adjudged criminals because they sit, or claim the right to sit, in the same public coach on a public highway.

The arbitrary separation of citizens, on the basis of race, while they are on a public highway, is a badge of servitude wholly inconsistent with the civil freedom and the equality before the law established by the Constitution. It cannot be justified upon any legal grounds.

If evils will result from the commingling of the two races upon public highways established for the benefit of all, they will be infinitely less than those that will surely come from state legislation regulating the enjoyment of civil rights upon the basis of race. We boast of the freedom enjoyed by our people above all other peoples. But it is difficult to reconcile that boast with a state of the law which, practically, puts the brand of servitude and degradation upon a large class of our fellow-citizens, our equals before the law. The thin disguise of "equal" accommodations for passengers in railroad coaches will not mislead any one, nor atone for the wrong this day done.

The result of the whole matter is, that while this court has frequently adjudged, and at the present term has recognized the doctrine, that a State cannot, consistently with the Constitution of the United States, prevent white and black citizens, having the required qualifications for jury service, from sitting in the same jury box, it is now solemnly held that a State may prohibit white and black citizens from sitting in the same passenger coach on a public highway, or may require that they be separated by a "partition," when in the same passenger coach. May it not now be reasonably expected that astute men of the dominant race, who affect to be disturbed at the possibility that the integrity of the white race may be corrupted, or that its supremacy will be imperilled, by contact on public highways with black people, will endeavor to procure statutes requiring white and black jurors to be separated in the jury box by a "partition," and that, upon retiring from the court room to consult as to their verdict, such partition, if it be a moveable one, shall be taken to their consultation room, and set up in such way as to prevent black jurors from coming too close to their brother jurors of the white race. If the "partition" used in the court room happens to be stationary, provision could be made for screens with openings through which jurors of the two races could confer as to their verdict without coming into personal contact with each other. I cannot see but that, according to the principles this day announced, such state legislation, although conceived in hostility to, and enacted for the purpose of humiliating citizens of the United States of a particular race, would be held to be consistent with the Constitution.

I do not deem it necessary to review the decisions of state courts to which reference was made in argument. Some, and the most important, of them are wholly inapplicable, because rendered prior to the adoption of the last amendments of the Constitution, when colored people had very few rights which the dominant race felt obliged to respect. Others were made at a time when public opinion, in many localities, was dominated by the institution of slavery; when it would not have been safe to do justice to the black man;

and when, so far as the rights of blacks were concerned, race prejudice was, practically, the supreme law of the land. Those decisions cannot be guides in the era introduced by the recent amendments of the supreme law, which established universal civil freedom, gave citizenship to all born or naturalized in the United States and residing here, obliterated the race line from our systems of governments, National and State, and placed our free institutions upon the broad and sure foundation of the equality of all men before the law.

I am of opinion that the statute of Louisiana is inconsistent with the personal liberty of citizens, white and black, in that State, and hostile to both the spirit and letter of the Constitution of the United Sates. If laws of like character should be enacted in the several States of the Union, the effect would be in the highest degree mischievous. Slavery, as an institution tolerated by law would, it is true, have disappeared from our country, but there would remain a power in the States, by sinister legislation, to interfere with the full enjoyment of the blessings of freedom; to regulate civil rights, common to all citizens, upon the basis of race; and to place in a condition of legal inferiority a large body of American citizens, now constituting a part of the political community called the People of the United States, for whom, and by whom through representatives, our government is administered. Such a system is inconsistent with the guarantee given by the Constitution to each State of a republican form of government, and may be stricken down by Congressional action, or by the courts in the discharge of their solemn duty to maintain the supreme law of the land, anything in the constitution or laws of any State to the contrary notwithstanding.

For the reasons stated, I am constrained to withhold my assent from the opinion and judgment of the majority.

BROWN et al. v. BOARD OF EDUCATION et al.

1952 HEARING

97 L.Ed. 3

73 S.Ct. 1

344 U.S .1

BROWN et al. v. BOARD OF EDUCATION
OF TOPEKA, SHAWNEE COUNTY,
KAN., et al.

BRIGGS et al. v. ELLIOTT et al.

DAVIS et al. v. COUNTY SCHOOL BOARD
OF PRINCE EDWARD COUNTY,
VA., et al.

Nos. 8, 101, 191.

Decided Oct. 8, 1952.

Per Curiam

In two appeals now pending, No. 8, Brown et al. v. Board of Education of Topeka et al., and No. 101, Briggs et al. v. Elliott et al., the appellants challenge, respectively, the constitutionality of a statute of Kansas, and a statute and the constitution of South Carolina, which provide for segregation in the schools of these states. D.C., 98 F.Supp. 797, D.C., 103 F.Supp. 920. Appellants allege that segregation is, *per se*, a violation of the Fourteenth Amendment. Argument in these cases has heretofore been set for the week of October 13, 1952.

In No. 191, Davis et al. v. County School Board of Prince Edward County et al., the appellants have filed a Statement of Jurisdiction raising the same issue in respect to a statute and the constitution of Virginia. D.C., 103 F.Supp. 337. Appellees in the Davis case have called attention to the similarity between it and the Briggs and Brown cases; by motion they have asked the Court to take necessary action to have all three cases argued together.

131

This Court takes judicial note of a fourth case, which is pending in the United States Court of Appeals for the District of Columbia Circuit, Bolling et al. v. Sharpe et al., No. 11,018 on that court's docket. In that case, the appellants challenge the appellees' refusal to admit certain Negro appellants to a segregated white school, in the District of Columbia; they allege that appellees have taken such action pursuant to certain Acts of Congress; they allege that such action is a violation of the Fifth Amendment of the Constitution.

The Court is of the opinion that the nature of the issue posed in those appeals now before the Court involving the Fourteenth Amendment, and also the effect of any decision which it may render in those cases, are such that it would be well to consider, simultaneously, the constitutional issues posed in the case of Bolling v. Sharpe.

To the end that arguments may be heard together in all four of these cases, the Court will continue the Brown and Briggs cases on its docket. Probable jurisdiction is noted in Davis v. County School Board of Prince Edward County. Arguments will be heard in these three cases at the first argument session in December.

The Court will entertain a petition for certiorari in the case of Bolling v. Sharpe, 28 U.S.C. §§ 1254(1), 2101(e), 28 U.S.C.A. §§ 1254(1), 2101(e), which if presented and granted will afford opportunity for argument of the case immediately following the arguments in the three appeals now pending. It is so ordered.

Cases continued.

Mr. Justice DOUGLAS dissents from postponing argument and decision in the three cases presently here for Bolling v. Sharpe, in the United States Court of Appeals for the District of Columbia Circuit.

BROWN et al. v. BOARD OF EDUCATION et al.
1954 DECISION

98 L.Ed. 873
74 S.Ct. 686
347 U.S. 483

BROWN et al. v. BOARD OF EDUCATION
OF TOPEKA, SHAWNEE COUNTY,
KAN., et al.

BRIGGS et al. v. ELLIOTT et al.

DAVIS et al. v. COUNTY SCHOOL BOARD
OF PRINCE EDWARD COUNTY,
VA., et al.

GEBHART et al. v. BELTON et al.

Nos. 1, 2, 4, 10.

Decided May 17, 1954.

Mr. Chief Justice WARREN delivered the opinion of the Court.

These cases come to us from the States of Kansas, South Carolina, Virginia, and Delaware. They are premised on different facts and different local conditions, but a common legal question justifies their consideration together in this consolidated opinion.[1]

----

[1] In the Kansas case, Brown v. Board of Education, the plaintiffs are Negro children of elementary school age residing in Topeka. They brought this action in the United States District Court for the District of Kansas to enjoin enforcement of a Kansas statute which permits, but does not require, cities of more than 15,000 population to maintain separate school facilities for Negro and white students. Kan.Gen.Stat.1949, § 72–1724. Pursuant to that authority, the Topeka Board of Education elected to establish segregated elementary schools. Other public schools in the community, however, are operated on a nonsegregated basis. The three-judge District Court, convened under 28 U.S.C. §§ 2281 and 2284, 28 U.S.C.A. §§ 2281, 2284, found that segregation in public education has a detrimental effect upon Negro children, but denied relief on the ground that the Negro and white schools were substantially equal with respect to buildings, transportation, curricula,

and educational qualifications of teachers. 98 F.Supp. 797. The case is here on direct appeal under 28 U.S.C. § 1253, 28 U.S.C.A. § 1253.

In the South Carolina case, Briggs v. Elliott, the plaintiffs are Negro children of both elementary and high school age residing in Clarendon County. They brought this action in the United States District Court for the Eastern District of South Carolina to enjoin enforcement of provisions in the state constitution and statutory code which require the segregation of Negroes and whites in public schools. S.C.Const. Art. XI, § 7; S.C.Code 1942, § 5377. The three-judge District Court, convened under 28 U.S.C. §§ 2281 and 2284, 28 U.S.C.A. §§ 2281, 2284, denied the requested relief. The court found that the Negro schools were inferior to the white schools and ordered the defendants to begin immediately to equalize the facilities. But the court sustained the validity of the contested provisions and denied the plaintiffs admission to the white schools during the equalization program. 98 F.Supp. 529. This Court vacated the District Court's judgment and remanded the case for the purpose of obtaining the court's views on a report filed by the defendants concerning the progress made in the equalization program. 342 U.S. 350, 72 S.Ct. 327, 96 L.Ed. 392. On remand, the District Court found that substantial equality had been achieved except for buildings and that the defendants were proceeding to rectify this inequality as well. 103 F.Supp. 920. The case is again here on direct appeal under 28 U.S.C. § 1253, 28 U.S.C.A. § 1253.

In the Virginia case, Davis v. County School Board, the plaintiffs are Negro children of high school age residing in Prince Edward County. They brought this action in the United States District Court for the Eastern District of Virginia to enjoin enforcement of provisions in the state constitution and statutory code which require the segregation of Negroes and whites in public schools. Va.Const. § 140; Va.Code 1950, § 22–221. The three-judge District Court, convened under 28 U.S.C. §§ 2281 and 2284, 28 U.S.C.A. §§ 2281, 2284, denied the requested relief. The court found the Negro school inferior in physical plant, curricula, and transportation, and ordered the defendants forthwith to provide substantially equal curricula and transportation and to "proceed with all reasonable diligence and dispatch to remove" the inequality in physical plant. But, as in the South Carolina case, the court sustained the validity of the contested provisions and denied the plaintiffs admission to the white schools during the equalization program. 103 F.Supp. 337. The case is here on direct appeal under 28 U.S.C. § 1253, 28 U.S.C.A. § 1253.

In the Delaware case, Gebhart v. Belton, the plaintiffs are Negro children of both elementary and high school age residing in New Castle County. They brought this action in the Delaware Court of Chancery to enjoin enforcement of provisions in the state constitution and statutory code which require the segregation of Negroes and whites in public schools. Del.Const. Art. X, § 2; Del.Rev.Code, 1935, § 2631, 14 Del.C. § 141. The Chancellor gave judgment for the plaintiffs and ordered their immediate admission to schools previously attended only by white children, on the ground that the Negro schools were inferior with respect to teacher training, pupil-teacher ratio, extracurricular activities, physical plant, and time and distance involved in

In each of the cases, minors of the Negro race, through their legal representatives, seek the aid of the courts in obtaining admission to the public schools of their community on a nonsegregated basis. In each instance, they have been denied admission to schools attended by white children under laws requiring or permitting segregation according to race. This segregation was alleged to deprive the plaintiffs of the equal protection of the laws under the Fourteenth Amendment. In each of the cases other than the Delaware case, a three-judge federal district court denied relief to the plaintiffs on the so-called "separate but equal" doctrine announced by this Court in Plessy v. Ferguson, 163 U.S. 537, 16 S.Ct. 1138, 41 L.Ed. 256. Under that doctrine, equality of treatment is accorded when the races are provided substantially equal facilities, even though these facilities be separate. In the Delaware case, the Supreme Court of Delaware adhered to that doctrine, but ordered that the plaintiffs be admitted to the white schools because of their superiority to the Negro schools.

The plaintiffs contend that segregated public schools are not "equal" and cannot be made "equal," and that hence they are deprived of the equal protection of the laws. Because of the obvious importance of the question presented, the Court took jurisdiction.[2] Argument was heard in the

---

travel. Del.Ch., 87 A.2d 862. The Chancellor also found that segregation itself results in an inferior education for Negro children (see note 10, *infra*), but did not rest his decision on that ground. 87 A.2d at page 865. The Chancellor's decree was affirmed by the Supreme Court of Delaware, which intimated, however, that the defendants might be able to obtain a modification of the decree after equalization of the Negro and white schools had been accomplished. 91 A.2d 137, 152. The defendants, contending only that the Delaware courts had erred in ordering the immediate admission of the Negro plaintiffs to the white schools, applied to this Court for certiorari. The writ was granted, 344 U.S. 891, 73 S.Ct. 213, 97 L.Ed. 689. The plaintiffs, who were successful below, did not submit a cross-petition.

[2] 344 U.S. 1, 73 S.Ct. 1, 97 L.Ed. 3, Id., 344 U.S. 141, 73 S.Ct. 124, 97 L.Ed. 152, Gebhart v. Belton, 344 U.S. 891, 73 S.Ct. 213, 97 L.Ed. 689.

1952 Term, and reargument was heard this Term on certain questions propounded by the Court.[3]

Reargument was largely devoted to the circumstances surrounding the adoption of the Fourteenth Amendment in 1868. It covered exhaustively consideration of the Amendment in Congress, ratification by the states, then existing practices in racial segregation, and the views of proponents and opponents of the Amendment. This discussion and our own investigation convince us that, although these sources cast some light, it is not enough to resolve the problem with which we are faced. At best, they are inconclusive. The most avid proponents of the post-War Amendments undoubtedly intended them to remove all legal distinctions among "all persons born or naturalized in the United States." Their opponents, just as certainly, were antagonistic to both the letter and the spirit of the Amendments and wished them to have the most limited effect. What others in Congress and the state legislatures had in mind cannot be determined with any degree of certainty.

An additional reason for the inconclusive nature of the Amendment's history, with respect to segregated schools, is the status of public education at that time.[4] In the South,

---

3 345 U.S. 972, 73 S.Ct. 1118, 97 L.Ed. 1388. The Attorney General of the United States participated both Terms as *amicus curiae*.

4 For a general study of the development of public education prior to the Amendment, see Butts and Cremin, A History of Education in American Culture (1953), Pts. I, II; Cubberley, Public Education in the United States (1934 ed.), cc. II–XII. School practices current at the time of the adoption of the Fourteenth Amendment are described in Butts and Crimin, supra, at 269–275; Cubberley, supra, at 288–339, 408–431; Knight, Public Education in the South (1922), cc. VIII, IX. See also H. Ex. Doc. No. 315, 41st Cong., 2d Sess. (1871). Although the demand for free public schools followed substantially the same pattern in both the North and the South, the development in the South did not begin to gain momentum until about 1850, some twenty years after that in the North. The reasons for the somewhat slower development in the South (e.g., the rural character of the South and the different regional attitudes toward state assistance) are well explained in Cubberley, supra, at 408–423. In the country as a whole, but particularly

the movement toward free common schools, supported by general taxation, had not yet taken hold. Education of white children was largely in the hands of private groups. Education of Negroes was almost nonexistent, and practically all of the race were illiterate. In fact, any education of Negroes was forbidden by law in some states. Today, in contrast, many Negroes have achieved outstanding success in the arts and sciences as well as in the business and professional world. It is true that public school education at the time of the Amendment had advanced further in the North, but the effect of the Amendment on Northern States was generally ignored in the congressional debates. Even in the North, the conditions of public education did not approximate those existing today. The curriculum was usually rudimentary; ungraded schools were common in rural areas; the school term was but three months a year in many states; and compulsory school attendance was virtually unknown. As a consequence, it is not surprising that there should be so little in the history of the Fourteenth Amendment relating to its intended effect on public education.

In the first cases in this Court construing the Fourteenth Amendment, decided shortly after its adoption, the Court interpreted it as proscribing all state-imposed discriminations against the Negro race.[5] The doctrine of "separate

---

in the South, the War virtually stopped all progress in public education. Id., at 427–428. The low status of Negro education in all sections of the country, both before and immediately after the War, is described in Beale, A History of Freedom of Teaching in American Schools (1941), 112–132, 175–195. Compulsory school attendance laws were not generally adopted until after the ratification of the Fourteenth Amendment, and it was not until 1918 that such laws were in force in all the states. Cubberley, supra, at 563–565.

[5] In re Slaughter-House Cases, 1873, 16 Wall. 36, 67–72, 21 L.Ed. 394; Strauder v. West Virginia, 1880, 100 U.S. 303, 307–308, 25 L.Ed. 664.

"It ordains that no State shall deprive any person of life, liberty, or property, without due process of law, or deny to any person within its jurisdiction the equal protection of the laws. What is this but declaring that the law in

but equal" did not make its appearance in this Court until 1896 in the case of Plessy v. Ferguson, supra, involving not education but transportation.[6] American courts have since labored with the doctrine for over half a century. In this Court, there have been six cases involving the "separate but equal" doctrine in the field of public education.[7] In Cumming v. Board of Education of Richmond County, 175 U.S. 528, 20 S.Ct. 197, 44 L.Ed. 262, and Gong Lum v. Rice, 275 U.S. 78, 48 S.Ct. 91, 72 L.Ed. 172, the validity of the doctrine itself was not challenged.[8] In more recent cases, all on the graduate school level, inequality was found in that specific benefits enjoyed by white students were denied to Negro students of the same educational qualifications. State of

---

the States shall be the same for the black as for the white; that all persons, whether colored or white, shall stand equal before the laws of the States, and, in regard to the colored race, for whose protection the amendment was primarily designed, that no discrimination shall be made against them by law because of their color? The words of the amendment, it is true, are prohibitory, but they contain a necessary implication of a positive immunity, or right, most valuable to the colored race,—the right to exemption from unfriendly legislation against them distinctively as colored,—exemption from legal discriminations, implying inferiority in civil society, lessening the security of their enjoyment of the rights which others enjoy, and discriminations which are steps towards reducing them to the condition of a subject race."

See also State of Virginia v. Rives, 1879, 100 U.S. 313, 318, 25 L.Ed. 667; Ex parte Vrginia, 1879, 100 U.S. 339, 344–345, 25 L.Ed. 676.

[6] The doctrine apparently originated in Roberts v. City of Boston, 1850, 5 Cush. 198, 59 Mass. 198, 206, upholding school segregation against attack as being violative of a state constitutional guarantee of equality. Segregation in Boston public schools was eliminated in 1855. Mass. Acts 1855, c. 256. But elsewhere in the North segregation in public education has persisted in some communities until recent years. It is apparent that such segregation has long been a nationwide problem, not merely one of sectional concern.

[7] See also Berea College v. Kentucky, 1908, 211 U.S. 45, 29 S.Ct. 33, 53 L.Ed. 81.

[8] In the Cumming case, Negro taxpayers sought an injunction requiring the defendant school board to discontinue the operation of a high school for white children until the board resumed operation of a high school for Negro children. Similarly, in the Gong Lum case, the plaintiff, a child of Chinese descent, contended only that state authorities had misapplied the doctrine by classifying him with Negro children and requiring him to attend a Negro school.

Missouri ex rel. Gaines v. Canada, 305 U.S. 337, 59 S.Ct. 232, 83 L.Ed. 208; Sipuel v. Board of Regents of University of Oklahoma, 332 U.S. 631, 68 S.Ct. 299, 92 L.Ed. 247; Sweatt v. Painter, 339 U.S. 629, 70 S.Ct. 848, 94 L.Ed. 1114; McLaurin v. Oklahoma State Regents, 339 U.S. 637, 70 S.Ct. 851, 94 L.Ed. 1149. In none of these cases was it necessary to re-examine the doctrine to grant relief to the Negro plaintiff. And in Sweatt v. Painter, supra, the Court expressly reserved decision on the question whether Plessy v. Ferguson should be held inapplicable to public education.

In the instant cases, that question is directly presented. Here, unlike Sweatt v. Painter, there are findings below that the Negro and white schools involved have been equalized, or are being equalized, with respect to buildings, curricula, qualifications and salaries of teachers, and other "tangible" factors.[9] Our decision, therefore, cannot turn on merely a comparison of these tangible factors in the Negro and white schools involved in each of the cases. We must look instead to the effect of segregation itself on public education.

In approaching this problem, we cannot turn the clock back to 1868 when the Amendment was adopted, or even to 1896 when Plessy v. Ferguson was written. We must consider public education in the light of its full development and its present place in American life throughout the Nation. Only in this way can it be determined if segregation in public schools deprives these plaintiffs of the equal protection of the laws.

Today, education is perhaps the most important function

---

[9] In the Kansas case, the court below found substantial equality as to all such factors. 98 F.Supp. 797, 798. In the South Carolina case, the court below found that the defendants were proceeding "promptly and in good faith to comply with the court's decree." 103 F.Supp. 920, 921. In the Virginia case, the court below noted that the equalization program was already "afoot and progressing," 103 F.Supp. 337, 341; since then, we have been advised, in the Virginia Attorney General's brief on reargument, that the program has now been completed. In the Delaware case, the court below similarly noted that the state's equalization program was well under way. 91 A.2d 137, 139.

of state and local governments. Compulsory school attendance laws and the great expenditures for education both demonstrate our recognition of the importance of education to our democratic society. It is required in the performance of our most basic public responsibilities, even service in the armed forces. It is the very foundation of good citizenship. Today it is a principal instrument in awakening the child to cultural values, in preparing him for later professional training, and in helping him to adjust normally to his environment. In these days, it is doubtful that any child may reasonably be expected to succeed in life if he is denied the opportunity of an education. Such an opportunity, where the state has undertaken to provide it, is a right which must be made available to all on equal terms.

We come then to the question presented: Does segregation of children in public schools solely on the basis of race, even though the physical facilities and other "tangible" factors may be equal, deprive the children of the minority group of equal educational opportunities? We believe that it does.

In Sweatt v. Painter, supra [339 U.S. 629, 70 S.Ct. 850], in finding that a segregated law school for Negroes could not provide them equal educational opportunities, this Court relied in large part on "those qualities which are incapable of objective measurement but which make for greatness in a law school." In McLaurin v. Oklahoma State Regents, supra [339 U.S. 637, 70 S.Ct. 853], the Court, in requiring that a Negro admitted to a white graduate school be treated like all other students, again resorted to intangible considerations: "* * * his ability to study, to engage in discussions and exchange views with other students, and, in general, to learn his profession." Such considerations apply with added force to children in grade and high schools. To separate them from others of similar age and qualifications solely because of their race generates a feeling of inferiority as to their status in the community that may affect their hearts and minds in a way unlikely ever to be undone. The effect of this separation on their educational opportunities was well stated by a finding in the Kansas case by a court which nevertheless felt compelled to rule against the Negro plaintiffs:

> Segregation of white and colored children in public schools has a detrimental effect upon the colored children. The impact is greater when it has the sanction of the law; for the policy of separating the races is usually interpreted as denoting the inferiority of the negro group. A sense of inferiority affects the motivation of a child to learn. Segregation with the sanction of law, therefore, has a tendency to [retard] the educational and mental development of Negro children and to deprive them of some of the benefits they would receive in a racial[ly] integrated school system.[10]

Whatever may have been the extent of psychological knowledge at the time of Plessy v. Ferguson, this finding is amply supported by modern authority.[11] Any language in Plessy v. Ferguson contrary to this finding is rejected.

We conclude that in the field of public education the doctrine of "separate but equal" has no place. Separate educational facilities are inherently unequal. Therefore, we

---

[10] A similar finding was made in the Delaware case: "I conclude from the testimony that in our Delaware society, State-imposed segregation in education itself results in the Negro children, as a class, receiving educational opportunities which are substantially inferior to those available to white children otherwise similarly situated." 87 A.2d 862, 865.

[11] K. B. Clark, Effect of Prejudice and Discrimination on Personality Development (Midcentury White House Conference on Children and Youth, 1950); Witmer and Kotinsky, Personality in the Making (1952), c. VI; Deutscher and Chein, The Psychological Effects of Enforced Segregation: A Survey of Social Science Opinion, 26 J.Psychol. 259 (1948); Chein, What are the Psychological Effects of Segregation Under Conditions of Equal Facilities?, 3 Int. J. Opinion and Attitude Res. 229 (1949); Brameld, Educational Costs, in Discrimination and National Welfare (MacIver, ed., 1949), 44–48; Frazier, The Negro in the United States (1949), 674–681. And see generally Myrdal, An American Dilemma (1944).

hold that the plaintiffs and others similarly situated for whom the actions have been brought are, by reason of the segregation complained of, deprived of the equal protection of the laws guaranteed by the Fourteenth Amendment. This disposition makes unnecessary any discussion whether such segregation also violates the Due Process Clause of the Fourteenth Amendment.[12]

Because these are class actions, because of the wide applicability of this decision, and because of the great variety of local conditions, the formulation of decrees in these cases presents problems of considerable complexity. On reargument, the consideration of appropriate relief was necessarily subordinated to the primary question—the constitutionality of segregation in public education. We have now announced that such segregation is a denial of the equal protection of the laws. In order that we may have the full assistance of the parties in formulating decrees, the cases will be restored to the docket, and the parties are requested to present further argument on Questions 4 and 5 previously propounded by the Court for the reargument this Term.[13]

---

12 See Bolling v. Sharpe, 347 U.S. 497, 74 S.Ct. 693, concerning the Due Process Clause of the Fifth Amendment.

13 "4. Assuming it is decided that segregation in public schools violates the Fourteenth Amendment

"(a) would a decree necessarily follow providing that, within the limits set by normal geographic school districting, Negro children should forthwith be admitted to schools of their choice, or

"(b) may this Court, in the exercise of its equity powers, permit an effective gradual adjustment to be brought about from existing segregated systems to a system not based on color distinctions?

"5. On the assumption on which questions 4(a) and (b) are based, and assuming further that this Court will exercise its equity powers to the end described in question 4(b),

"(a) should this Court formulate detailed decrees in these cases;

"(b) if so, what specific issues should the decrees reach;

"(c) should this Court appoint a special master to hear evidence with a view to recommending specific terms for such decrees;

"(d) should this Court remand to the courts of first instance with directions to frame decrees in these cases, and if so what general directions should

The Attorney General of the United States is again invited to participate. The Attorneys General of the states requiring or permitting segregation in public education will also be permitted to appear as *amici curiae* upon request to do so by September 15, 1954, and submission of briefs by October 1, 1954.[14]

It is so ordered.

Cases ordered restored to docket for further argument on question of appropriate decrees.

---

the decrees of this Court include and what procedures should the courts of first instance follow in arriving at the specific terms of more detailed decrees?"

[14] See Rule 42, Revised Rules of this Court, effective July 1, 1954, 28 U.S.C.A.

TITLE II OF THE
1964 CIVIL RIGHTS ACT:

KNOWN AS THE "PUBLIC ACCOMMODATION SECTION"

(This is not the entire 1964 Civil Rights Act but only a portion of it, to wit: Title II.)

TITLE II—INJUNCTIVE RELIEF AGAINST DISCRIMINATION IN PLACES OF PUBLIC ACCOMMODATION

SEC. 201. (a) All persons shall be entitled to the full and equal enjoyment of the goods, services, facilities, privileges, advantages, and accommodations of any place of public accommodation, as defined in this section, without discrimination or segregation on the ground of race, color, religion, or national origin.

(b) Each of the following establishments which serves the public is a place of public accommodation within the meaning of this title if its operations affect commerce, or if discrimination or segregation by it is supported by State action:

(1) any inn, hotel, motel, or other establishment which provides lodging to transient guests, other than an establishment located within a building which contains not more than five rooms for rent or hire and which is actually occupied by the proprietor of such establishment as his residence;

(2) any restaurant, cafeteria, lunchroom, lunch counter, soda fountain, or other facility principally engaged in selling food for consumption on the premises, including, but not limited to, any such facility located on the premises of any retail establishment; or any gasoline station;

(3) any motion picture house, theater, concert hall,

144

sports arena, stadium or other place of exhibition or entertainment; and

(4) any establishment (A)(i) which is physically located within the premises of any establishment otherwise covered by this subsection, or (ii) within the premises of which is physically located any such covered establishment, and (B) which holds itself out as serving patrons of such covered establishment.

(c) The operations of an establishment affect commerce within the meaning of this title if (1) it is one of the establishments described in paragraph (1) of subsection (b); (2) in the case of an establishment described in paragraph (2) of subsection (b), it serves or offers to serve interstate travelers or a substantial portion of the food which it serves, or gasoline or other products which it sells, has moved in commerce; (3) in the case of an establishment described in paragraph (3) of subsection (b), it customarily presents films, performances, athletic teams, exhibitions, or other sources of entertainment which move in commerce; and (4) in the case of an establishment described in paragraph (4) of subsection (b), it is physically located within the premises of, or there is physically located within its premises, an establishment the operations of which affect commerce within the meaning of this subsection. For purposes of this section, "commerce" means travel, trade, traffic, commerce, transportation, or communication among the several States, or between the District of Columbia and any State, or between any foreign country or any territory or possession and any State or the District of Columbia, or between points in the same State but through any other State or the District of Columbia or a foreign country.

(d) Discrimination or segregation by an establishment is supported by State action within the meaning of this title if such discrimination or segregation (1) is carried on under color of any law, statute, ordinance, or regulation; or (2) is carried on under color of any custom or usage required or enforced by officials of the State or political subdivision thereof; or (3) is required by action of the State or political subdivision thereof.

(e) The provisions of this title shall not apply to a private club or other establishment not in fact open to the public, except to the extent that the facilities of such establishment are made available to the customers or patrons of an establishment within the scope of subsection (b).

SEC. 202. All persons shall be entitled to be free, at any establishment or place, from discrimination or segregation of any kind on the ground of race, color, religion, or national origin, if such discrimination or segregation is or purports to be required by any law, statute, ordinance, regulation, rule, or order of a State or any agency or political subdivision thereof.

SEC. 203. No person shall (a) withhold, deny, or attempt to withhold or deny, or deprive or attempt to deprive, any person of any right or privilege secured by section 201 or 202, or (b) intimidate, threaten, or coerce, or attempt to intimidate, threaten, or coerce any person with the purpose of interfering with any right or privilege secured by section 201 or 202, or (c) punish or attempt to punish any person for exercising or attempting to exercise any right or privilege secured by section 201 or 202.

SEC. 204. (a) Whenever any person has engaged or there are reasonable grounds to believe that any person is about to engage in any act or practice prohibited by section 203, a civil action for preventive relief, including an application for a permanent or temporary injunction, restraining order, or other order, may be instituted by the person aggrieved and, upon timely application, the court may, in its discretion, permit the Attorney General to intervene in such civil action if he certifies that the case is of general public importance. Upon application by the complainant and in such circumstances as the court may deem just, the court may appoint an attorney for such complainant and may authorize the commencement of the civil action without the payment of fees, costs, or security.

(b) In any action commenced pursuant to this title, the court, in its discretion, may allow the prevailing party, other than the United States, a reasonable attorney's fee as part of the costs, and the United States shall be liable for costs the same as a private person.

(c) In the case of an alleged act or practice prohibited by this title which occurs in a State, or political subdivision of a State, which has a State or local law prohibiting such act or practice and establishing or authorizing a State or local authority to grant or seek relief from such practice or to institute criminal proceedings with respect thereto upon receiving notice thereof, no civil action may be brought under subsection (a) before the expiration of thirty days after written notice of such alleged act or practice has been given to the appropriate State or local authority by registered mail or in person, provided that the court may stay proceedings in such civil action pending the termination of State or local enforcement proceedings.

(d) In the case of an alleged act or practice prohibited by this title which occurs in a State, or political subdivision of a State, which has no State or local law prohibiting such act or practice, a civil action may be brought under subsection (a): *Provided.* That the court may refer the matter to the Community Relations Service established by title X of this Act for as long as the court believes there is a reasonable possibility of obtaining voluntary compliance, but for not more than sixty days: *Provided further.* That upon expiration of such sixty-day period, the court may extend such period for an additional period, not to exceed a cumulative total of one hundred and twenty days, if it believes there then exists a reasonable possibility of securing voluntary compliance.

SEC. 205. The Service is authorized to make a full investigation of any complaint referred to it by the court under section 204(d) and may hold such hearings with respect thereto as may be necessary. The Service shall conduct any hearings with respect to any such complaint in executive session, and shall not release any testimony given therein except by agreement of all parties involved in the complaint with the permission of the court, and the Service shall endeavor to bring about a voluntary settlement between the parties.

SEC. 206. (a) Whenever the Attorney General has reasonable cause to believe that any person or group of persons is engaged in a pattern or practice of resistance to the full enjoyment of any of the rights secured by this title, and that the pattern or practice is of such a nature and is intended to deny the full exercise of the rights herein described, the Attorney General may bring a civil action in the appropriate district court of the United States by filing with it a complaint (1) signed by him (or in his absence, the Acting Attorney General), (2) setting forth facts pertaining to such pattern or practice, and (3) requesting such preventive relief, including an application for a permanent or temporary injunction, restraining order or other order against the person or persons responsible for such pattern or practice, as he deems necessary to insure the full enjoyment of the rights herein described.

(b) In any such proceeding the Attorney General may file with the clerk of such court a request that a court of three judges be convened to hear and determine the case. Such request by the Attorney General shall be accompanied by a certificate that, in his opinion, the case is of general public importance. A copy of the certificate and request for a three-judge court shall be immediately furnished by such clerk to the chief judge of the circuit (or in his absence, the presiding circuit judge of the circuit) in which the case is pending. Upon receipt of the copy of such request it shall be the duty of the chief judge of the circuit or the presiding circuit judge, as the case may be, to designate immediately three judges in such circuit, of whom at least one shall be a circuit judge and another of whom shall be a district judge of the court in which the proceeding was instituted, to hear and determine such case, and it shall be the duty of the judges so designated to assign the case for hearing at the earliest practicable date, to participate in the hearing and determination thereof, and to cause the case to be in every way expedited. An appeal from the final judgment of such court will lie to the Supreme Court.

In the event the Attorney General fails to file such a request in any such proceeding, it shall be the duty of the chief judge of the district (or in his absence, the acting chief judge) in which the case is pending immediately to designate a judge in such district to hear and determine the case. In the event that no judge in the district is available to hear and determine the case, the chief judge of the district, or the acting chief judge, as the case may be, shall certify this fact to the chief judge of the circuit (or in his absence, the acting chief judge) who shall then designate a district or circuit judge of the circuit to hear and determine the case.

It shall be the duty of the judge designated pursuant to this section to assign the case for hearing at the earliest practicable date and to cause the case to be in every way expedited.

Sec. 207. (a) The district courts of the United States shall have jurisdiction of proceedings instituted pursuant to this title and shall exercise the same without regard to whether the aggrieved party shall have exhausted any administrative or other remedies that may be provided by law.

(b) The remedies provided in this title shall be the exclusive means of enforcing the rights based on this title, but nothing in this title shall preclude any individual or any State or local agency from asserting any right based on any other Federal or State law not inconsistent with this title, including any statute or ordinance requiring nondiscrimination in public establishments or accommodations, or from pursuing any remedy, civil or criminal, which may be available for the vindication or enforcement of such right.

THE GENOVESE CASE

37 Who Saw Murder Didn't Call the Police[*]

APATHY AT STABBING OF QUEENS
WOMAN SHOCKS INSPECTOR

By Martin Gansberg

For more than half an hour [sic] respectable, law-abiding citizens in Queens watched a killer stalk and stab a woman in three separate attacks in Kew Gardens.

Twice the sound of their voices and the sudden glow of their bedroom lights interrupted him and frightened him off. Each time he returned, sought her out and stabbed her again. Not one person telephoned the police during the assault, one witness called after the woman was dead.

That was two weeks ago today. But Assistant Chief Inspector Frederick M. Lussen, in charge of the borough's detectives and a veteran of 25 years of homicide investigations, is still shocked.

He can give a matter-of-fact recitation of many murders. But the Kew Gardens slaying baffles him—not because it is a murder, but because the "good people" failed to call the police.

"As we have reconstructed the crime," he said, "the assailant had three chances to kill this woman during a 35-minute period. He returned twice to complete the job. If we had been called when he first attacked, the woman might not be dead now."

This is what the police say happened beginning at 3:20 A.M. in the staid, middle-class, tree-lined Austin Street area:

Twenty-eight-year-old Catherine Genovese, who was called Kitty by almost everyone in the neighborhood, was returning home from her job as manager of a bar in Hollis. She parked her red Fiat in a lot adjacent to the Kew Gardens Long Island Rail Road Station, facing Mowbray Place. Like many residents of the neighborhood, she had parked there day after day since her arrival from Connecticut a year ago, although the railroad frowns on the practice.

She turned off the lights of her car, locked the door and started to walk the 100 feet to the entrance of her apartment at 82–70 Austin Street, which is in a Tudor building, with stores on the first floor and apartments on the second.

The entrance to the apartment is in the rear of the building because the front is rented to retail stores. At night the quiet neighborhood is shrouded in the slumbering darkness that marks most residential areas.

Miss Genovese noticed a man at the far end of the lot, near a seven-story apartment house at 82–40 Austin Street. She halted. Then, nervously, she headed up

* *New York Times,* March 27, 1964, pp. 1, 38. © 1964 by The New York Times Company. Reprinted by permission.

Austin Street toward Lefferts Boulevard, where there is a call box to the 102nd Police Precinct in nearby Richmond Hill.

"He Stabbed Me."

She got as far as a street light in front of a bookstore before the man grabbed her. She screamed. Lights went on in the 10-story apartment house at 82–67 Austin Street, which faces the bookstore. Windows slid open and voices punctured the early-morning stillness.

Miss Genovese screamed: "Oh, my God, he stabbed me! Please help me! Please help me "

From one of the upper windows in the apartment house, a man called down: "Let that girl alone!"

The assailant looked up at him, shrugged and walked down Austin Street toward a white sedan parked a short distance away. Miss Genovese struggled to her feet.

Lights went out. The killer returned to Miss Genovese, now trying to make her way around the side of the building by the parking lot to get to her apartment. The assailant stabbed her again.

"I'm dying!" she shrieked. "I'm dying!"

A City Bus Passed

Windows were opened again, and lights went on in many apartments. The assailant got into his car and drove away. Miss Genovese staggered to her feet. A city bus, Q–10, the Lefferts Boulevard line to Kennedy International Airport, passed. It was 3:35 A.M.

The assailant returned. By then Miss Genovese had crawled to the back of the building, where the freshly painted brown doors to the apartment house held out hope of safety. The killer tried the first door; she wasn't there. At the second door, 82–62 Austin Street, he saw her slumped on the floor at the foot of the stairs. He stabbed her a third time—fatally.

It was 3:50 by the time the police received their first call, from a man who was a neighbor of Miss Genovese. In two minutes they were at the scene. The neighbor, a 70-year-old woman and another woman were the only persons on the street. Nobody else came forward.

The man explained that he had called the police after much deliberation. He had phoned a friend in Nassau County for advice and then he had crossed the roof of the building to the apartment of the elderly woman to get her to make the call.

"I didn't want to get involved," he sheepishly told the police.

Suspect Is Arrested

Six days later, the police arrested Winston Moseley, a 29-year-old business-machine operator, and charged him with the homicide. Moseley had no previous record. He is married, has two children and owns a home at 133–19 Sutter Avenue, South

Ozone Park, Queens. On Wednesday, a court committed him to Kings County Hospital for psychiatric observation.

When questioned by the police, Moseley also said that he had slain Mrs. Annie May Johnson, 24, of 146–12 133d Avenue, Jamaica, on Feb. 29 and Barbara Kralik, 15, of 174–17 140th Avenue, Springfield Gardens, last July. In the Kralik case, the police are holding Alvin L. Mitchell, who is said to have confessed that slaying.

The police stressed how simple it would have been to have gotten in touch with them. "A phone call," said one of the detectives, "would have done it." The police may be reached by dialing "0" for operator or SPring 7–3100.

The question of whether the witnesses can be held legally responsible in any way for failure to report the crime was put to the Police Department's legal bureau. There, a spokesman said:

"There is no legal responsibility, with few exceptions, for any citizens to report a crime."

Statutes Explained

Under the statutes of the city, he said, a witness to a suspicious or violent death must report it to the medical examiner. Under state law, a witness cannot withhold information in a kidnapping.

Today witnesses from the neighborhood, which is made up of one-family homes in the $35,000 to $60,000 range with the exception of the two apartment houses near the railroad station, find it difficult to explain why they didn't call the police.

Lieut. Bernard Jacobs, who handled the investigation by the detectives, said:

"It is one of the better neighborhoods. There are few reports of crimes. You only get the usual complaints about boys playing or garbage cans being turned over."

The police said most persons had told them they had been afraid to call, but had given meaningless answers when asked what they had feared.

"We can understand the reticence of people to become involved in an area of violence," Lieutenant Jacobs said, "but where they are in their homes near phones, why should they be afraid to call the police?"

He said his men were able to piece together what happened— and capture the suspect—because the residents furnished all the information when detectives rang doorbells during the days following the slaying.

"But why didn't someone call us that night?" he asked unbelievingly.

Witnesses—some of them unable to believe what they had allowed to happen—told a reporter why.

A housewife, knowingly if quite casual, said, "We thought it was a lover's quarrel." A husband and wife both said,

"Frankly, we were afraid." They seemed aware of the fact that events might have been different. A distraught woman, wiping her hands in her apron, said, "I didn't want my husband to get involved."

One couple, now willing to talk about that night, said they heard the first screams. The husband looked thoughtfully at the bookstore where the killer first grabbed Miss Genovese.

"We went to the window to see what was happening," he said, "but the light from our bedroom made it difficult to see the street." The wife, still apprehensive, added: "I put out the light and we were able to see better."

Asked why they hadn't called the police, she shrugged and replied, "I don't know."

A man peeked out from a slight opening in the doorway to his apartment and rattled off an account of the killer's second attack. Why hadn't he called the police at the time? "I was tired," he said without emotion, "I went back to bed."

It was 4:25 A.M. when the ambulance arrived for the body of Miss Genovese. It drove off. "Then," a solemn police detective said, "the people came out."

APATHY IS PUZZLE IN QUEENS KILLING[*]

BEHAVIORAL SPECIALISTS HARD PUT TO EXPLAIN WITNESSES' FAILURE TO CALL POLICE

Interpretations Vary

SOME SAY TENDENCY NOT TO GET INVOLVED IS TYPICAL— OTHERS CALL IT UNCOMMON

By Charles Mohr

Expressions of shock and perplexity followed the disclosure yesterday that 37 witnesses to a murder in Queens had failed to report the crime to the police.

Experts in human behavior, such as psychiatrists and sociologists, seemed as hard put as anyone else to explain the inaction of the witnesses.

One sociologist called it "nonrational behavior."

The murder took place two weeks ago in the Austin Street area of Kew Gardens. Miss Catherine Genovese, 28 years old, was attacked three separate times, within a span of 35 minutes, by a man with a knife.

Miss Genovese's cries aroused a total of 38 of her neighbors, some of whom witnessed the stabbing from their apartment windows. One of them, after

* *New York Times,* March 28, 1964, pp. 21, 40. © 1964 by The New York Times Company. Reprinted by permission.

hesitation, did call the police, but by then she was dead.

Suspect Was Arrested

The police have since arrested a 29-year-old busines machine operator, Winston Moseley, and charged him with the murder.

Most of the witnesses, in attempting to explain their inaction, said they "did not want to get involved."

Walter Arm, Deputy Police Commissioner for Community Relations, said the case was "dramatic and shocking," but added that "this tendency to shy away from reporting crimes is a common one."

Mr. Arm announced that the police department would soon redistribute a leaflet called "Law and Order is a Two-Way Street," which exhorts citizens to "report all crime immediately" and to "report to the police all suspicions of criminal activity."

He said several hundred thousand copies of the leaflet had been distributed in the past because the department had long been concerned with the problem of public apathy in reporting crimes.

Bar Official Indignant

Leo J. Zimmerman, vice president of the Queens Bar Association, called the incident "outrageous" and said he was "profoundly shocked." He said he was not speaking on behalf of the bar association.

Mr. Zimmerman is organizing a "Law Day U.S." program to be held May 1 at the World's Fair Pavilion in response to a proclamation by President Johnson requesting that such ceremonies be held throughout the nation. Mr. Zimmerman said the Kew Gardens case showed the need for such programs to "indoctrinate the public with their responsibility" and to "fight this tendency to look the other way."

Psychiatrists, psychologists and sociologists assigned varying explanations and significance to the event.

Dr. Iago Galdston, a psychiatrist, said, "I would assign this to the effect of the megalopolis in which we live which makes closeness very difficult and leads to the alienation of the individual to the group."

He said he was "quite sure this never could have happened in a small community—the response would have been immediate and very human."

Leo Srole, a sociologist who is a professor at the Downstate Medical Center of New York State University, said the incident "goes to the heart of whether this is a community or a jungle." He suggested that when members of a society fail to defend each other they can come close to being "partners in crime."

But he added that he felt the incident was atypical and that it would be wrong to condemn New York as a community.

A psychiatrist, Dr. George Serban, who is on the staff of the

New York Mental Health Clinic, said the behavior of the witnesses was "typical" of middle-class groups in a city like New York.

"They have a nice life and what happens in the street, the life of the city itself, is a different matter," he said.

Fear Society Is Unjust

But he also said that such behavior reflected a "constant" feeling that "society is unjust to them."

"It's the air of all New York, the air of injustice," he said, "the feeling that you might get hurt if you act and that, whatever you do, you will be the one to suffer."

In a sermon last night, the Rev. Joseph C. Holbrook, Jr., of the Grace Reformed Church of Flatbush at Bedford Avenue and Lincoln Road, Brooklyn, said of the apathy toward the slaying that "our society is as sick as the one that crucified Jesus."

Dr. Renée Claire Fox, an associate professor of sociology at Barnard College, said, on the other hand, that the witnesses had shown what she called a "disaster syndrome" something like that seen in victims of sudden disasters such as tornadoes.

She said that witnessing a prolonged murder under their own windows had destroyed their feeling that the world was a "rational, orderly place" and as a result it "deeply shook their sense of safety and sureness." The result, she ventured, was an "affect denial" that caused them to withdraw psychologically from the event by ignoring it.

The Rev. Lawrence Durgin of Broadway Congregational Church pondered the incident and said he was reminded that in the parable of the Good Samaritan that "it was supposedly good people who passed by on the other side." He said shock grew out of the fact that we are "reluctant, perhaps, to admit that we haven't made much progress since then."

A theologian said: "I can't understand it. Maybe the depersonalizing here has gone farther than I had thought."

But then he added, "Don't quote me."

WHAT KIND OF PEOPLE ARE WE?[*]

Seldom has *The Times* published a more horrifying story than its account of how 38 respectable, law-abiding, middle-class Queens citizens watched a killer stalk his young woman victim

---

* *New York Times,* March 28, p. 18. © 1964 by The New York Times Company. Reprinted by permission.

in a parking lot in Kew Gardens over a half-hour period, without one of them making a call to the Police Department that might have saved her life. They would not have been exposed to any danger themselves; a simple telephone call in the privacy of their own homes was all that was needed. How incredible it is that such motivations as "I didn't want to get involved" deterred them from this act of simple humanity. Does residence in a great city destroy all sense of personal responsibility for one's neighbors? Who can explain such shocking indifference on the part of a cross section of our fellow New Yorkers? We regretfully admit that we do not know the answers.

Index

*This book has been set in 11 point Baskerville,
leaded 2 points, and in 9 point Baskerville,
leaded 2 points. Chapter numbers are 14 point
Baskerville Roman and chapter titles are in 14
point Baskerville italics. The size of the type
page is 23 x 38 picas.*